HERE
WE ARE
NOW

ALSO BY CHARLES R. CROSS

HERE
WE ARE
NOW

THE LASTING IMPACT OF KURT COBAIN

CHARLES R. CROSS

IT! BOOKS
AN IMPRINT OF HARPERCOLLINS PUBLISHERS

FIRST EDITION

Designed by Lorie Pagnozzi

Library of Congress Cataloging-in-Publication Data has been applied for.

ISBN 978-0-06-230821-4

14 15 16 17 18   OV/RRD   10 9 8 7 6 5 4 3 2 1

*TO ASHLAND, AND TO EVERY BOY AND GIRL WHO GOT OFF
THE SOFA, GRABBED A GUITAR, AND MADE IT TALK*

CONTENTS

PROLOGUE This Horrible Secret 1

ONE Holy Grail
Music & Influence 15

TWO Lamestain on My Wack Slacks
Grunge & Culture 43

THREE The $6,000 Cobain Trench Coat
Style & Fashion 65

FOUR The Perfect Seattle Moment
Aberdeen & Seattle 99

FIVE Happens Every Day
Addiction & Suicide 125

SIX The Last Rock Star
Legacy & Blue Eyes 161

Acknowledgments *179*

HERE
WE ARE
NOW

THIS HORRIBLE SECRET

On the morning of April 8, 1994, I was working in my office at the Seattle magazine *The Rocket* when I received a series of phone calls that would prove unforgettable. Two decades have passed since that day, but those moments still remain vivid and haunting. Sometimes they seem like part of a dream I can't escape, or forget. History was happening around me, but I didn't realize it in the moment. I can still remember my finger pressing the flashing Line One button on my office phone, but I had no clue, at the time, that this little red light would announce a sea change in both music and culture. Like all nightmares, I want it to end differently, but it doesn't. It can't; it's not a dream.

The first call to my desk that day came from radio station KXRX-FM. I occasionally did segments for them promoting local bands on the rise as the editor in chief of *The Rocket,* a Seattle music and entertainment magazine with a circulation of one hundred thousand. We championed Northwest bands and were the first publication to do cover stories on Nirvana, Soundgarden, Pearl Jam, Alice in Chains, and other Seattle groups. Even though I had a bird's-eye view of the Grunge explosion, I was as surprised as everyone else in town when our locals—many of them old friends who'd been playing around for years—became international superstars.

I expected this phone call to be about my next radio segment, but the tone of the DJ's voice wasn't that typical fast-talking cadence I was used to. Instead it was somber, deliberate, slightly alarmed.

"Do you think," the DJ asked, "there's a chance Kurt Cobain is dead?"

At that point, early on April 8, 1994, no one else had uttered those words. The radio station had received a phone call just moments before from a dispatcher at an electrician's office, tipping them off that one of their employees had found a body at Kurt's house. The caller had told the station, "You guys are going to owe me some pretty good Pink Floyd tickets for this." The police had just been summoned. The DJ thought that perhaps I might have more information on the identity of the body. "We haven't gone on the air with it yet," he said, "but do you think there's any chance it's Kurt?"

I said no. "It can't be him," I said. "It's got to be one of his drug buddies, who probably overdosed. It can't be Kurt. It just can't." My words were from a place of denial, of course, and felt false even as I said them. I was doing the kind of psychological bargaining that happens when you initially hear bad news. It was the same bargaining millions of Nirvana fans worldwide would be carrying out in a few hours. But at this moment in time, this news—this horrible secret—belonged only to the radio station, the electrical contractor, the police, and me.

It couldn't be Kurt, I repeated in my head. While his struggles with drugs were well known within the tight circle of Seattle music, some of his friends were in far deeper. Kurt had been arrested a few times the previous year, and his ongoing battle with heroin was no secret. But *that* body . . . it couldn't be his, because he couldn't be gone.

But he was.

Not long after that phone call, KXRX went on the air with a report that a body had been found at the Cobain mansion. All at once, all six of our phone lines at *The Rocket* lit up. Members of the media were calling to ask for comment, friends of Kurt's were calling to ask if we knew any details, and our own staff of freelancers was calling in to see if what they'd heard was true. The KXRX DJ later told me the horrible story of how Kurt's sister had phoned the station to say the body couldn't possibly be Kurt's because this was the first she was hearing about it, and news like that couldn't leak out before the family was notified. But that is exactly what happened. Kurt's family found out he was dead from a report on a radio station.

I was busy making phone calls to Nirvana's publicist, mutual friends, contacts at Geffen Records and Sub Pop, anyone I knew who might have more information. Frustratingly, nobody knew anything more than I did. I was doing what any magazine editor would have done, investigating leads. But this felt personal, too, because everyone in Seattle felt a connection to Kurt. It was even more personal at our magazine because not only had *The Rocket* given Nirvana their first press and covered everything they did from first single to stardom, but the band had advertised in our pages several times, looking for drummers. One of my regrets is that I cashed a check Kurt wrote *The Rocket* for twenty bucks to pay for a classified ad when it was already clear that he was destined for fame. At *The Rocket*, there was a principle that we couldn't treat the bands we covered as stars and still retain the respect they had for us—journalists didn't ask for autographs or keep signed checks. Another connection with the band our magazine had was that Nirvana's logo—in the Century Condensed font—had been set on *The Rocket*'s typesetting machine. That original logo, which had already been slapped on millions of albums, first came out of a giant old type machine a few feet from my desk.

But back on that morning, April 8, 1994, there was no time for nostalgia. I needed immediate answers because I also had a job to do, and that job had become a lot more complicated in the last few hours. *The Rocket* was set to go to press that night, and we'd been waiting all week for an interview we'd been promised with a certain rock star, one Courtney Love. Hole was poised to release *Live Through This* the following week, and her publicist had set up numerous interviews for us, all of which had been postponed. And, as luck would have it, we had a phone interview with Courtney scheduled for the *very day* Kurt's body was found. A paste-up of our next cover of *The Rocket,* complete with a photo of Courtney and Hole, was sitting on our art director's desk. It was only later that I'd discover the reason Courtney kept missing our scheduled interviews; she was out searching for Kurt, who had escaped rehab. When the news came that the body at the Cobain house had in fact been identified as Kurt's, I had the surreal task of directing our art staff to take Courtney Love *off* the cover of *The Rocket* and put her now-deceased husband *on*.

Amid that deadline drama in my office, the phones never stopped ringing. I tried to juggle the calls while, with my staff, I chose an iconic Charles Peterson photo of Kurt for the cover. It showed him jumping high in the air, almost as if he was already no longer of this earth; it was perfect. Our first cover story on Nirvana had run with the headline NIRVANA INVADES BERLIN. That had been an easy headline to write. Nirvana was on the rise back then. But this time around, no string of words could sum up the loss. It was too big to put into words, really.

In the end, we used the airborne photo with no type other than our logo and the date.

And the phones just kept ringing and ringing. Many of the calls were from media who had never even covered Nirvana before, or had maybe mentioned "Grunge" in one article, and were now trying to create a story where there was nothing to report other than an obituary. The barrage of phone calls began to rattle our office receptionist. This was a woman who was usually so sure of herself that she once had the nerve to demand Courtney Love put out a cigarette when Courtney walked into our office smoking (Courtney dropped it on the carpet and rubbed it out with her shoe). But that April day, the endless phone calls had unnerved the receptionist, and I could hear that strain in her voice when she buzzed me for the thousandth time with another call. She didn't say who was waiting. She told me flatly, "Pick up line one." When I did, I heard a raspy sound I recognized immediately, but that didn't make it any less bizarre.

"This is Larry King, and you're on the radio live," said the voice on the line. "What is this thing called Grunge music?" I was speechless. His show was so desperate to get someone in Seattle to take their calls that they'd bypassed the normal protocols of putting in a request for an on-air interview first. I wasn't given a chance to say no. I had been cold-called, and now I was live on the radio with Larry King.

Only a few weeks before, I'd read a column from James Wolcott about Larry King and his constant seizing on celebrity death. One quote read, "Who elected Larry King America's grief counselor? We, the viewing public, did, by driving up his ratings whenever somebody famous passes." Now I was a pawn in Larry King's indelicate dance between legitimate news and ratings–driven scandal.

King kept on, undeterred by my silence, moving forward in his typical style of asking a series of questions without waiting for answers. "Tell us, just who was Kurt Cobain? Why Seattle? Why should we care? What about drugs?"

I muttered something; I don't recall what. Larry continued: "Why Kurt? Why Grunge music? Who was he? Why do people care?" This nightmare of a day was spiraling out of control and Larry King, of all people, was interrogating me.

And then, uncharacteristically, Larry King paused for a moment, and asked the one question that had significance. It was more to the point, and it had the kind of clarity that you find when the simplest question is asked instead of a more complicated one. It was the way that Larry King sometimes could end up being brilliant, finding the one truth amid the clutter.

"Tell me, Mr. Cross," Larry King said, "why did Kurt Cobain matter?"

I don't recall what I said to Larry King. Given that day's

madness, and the fact that Kurt's body lay under a coroner's drape just a few miles away, I'm sure I didn't properly answer the question. In some small way, this book is my attempt, twenty years later, to do so. The impact of any person's life is difficult to fully see on the day a life ends, but the long view offers a wider and more accurate vista.

My goal with these pages is to examine how in the long view Kurt's work and life affected music, fashion, gender roles, the way we treat suicide and drug addiction, the way his hometown views itself, and the very idea of Seattle in culture. In some of these arenas, his impact has been tremendous; in others, it's been subtle. Still, his twenty-seven years on this earth had ramifications. His legacy continues to evolve and to change. The reality is that in twenty years we haven't stopped talking about Kurt Cobain. He still matters to me, and, I would argue, he still matters to an entire generation.

Larry King never would have put it this way, but what I'm seeking to address is the eternal question of history: how do we measure the life of a man?

This is not a biography of Kurt Cobain. I've already done that with *Heavier Than Heaven* in 2001. That book was a third-person narrative of the events of Kurt's life. *Here We*

Are Now, in contrast, is my first-person analysis of what that life meant, and how that meaning can be quantified—when it can be at all. There were many places in *Heavier Than Heaven* where I could have inserted myself as a narrator because I witnessed events, or because I was part of them in some slight way. Doing so would have broken the reader's trance of experiencing history, though. *Here We Are Now* is not objective, and it brings forth my own intersections with this tale, before and after Kurt's death, my analysis of that history, and, in some places, the voices of a few other select experts.

I know there are some critics who have already suggested, and certainly will say of this book, that as a society we have talked enough about Kurt Cobain. Maybe. I don't seek to canonize Kurt, glorify him, or portray him as if he were some kind of God of Rock. Doing that is to take away his humanity, and to sketch him as he would never have wanted. As a human being, he often showed incredibly bad judgment and made choices that hurt many people who cared for him, his suicide being the most obvious example. But even Kurt's demons have had an impact on the larger culture over the past two decades; his suicide, for example, has been studied and written about extensively. It is without any doubt the most famous suicide of the last two decades. That suicide, as horrible as it was, had an impact on who "we"—as a culture—"are now."

At the very least, Nirvana's music touched the generation it was made for. The world has changed much since 1991 when *Nevermind* was released, but the influence of that album has only grown as the years pass. Technology has since turned the music industry upside down, fractionalized genres into smaller slices, and diminished the possibility of any rock act dominating the way Nirvana did. I would argue that no rock star since Kurt has had that same combination of talent, voice, lyric-writing skill, and charisma—another reason he is so significant, two decades after his death. The rarity of that magic combo is also part of the reason Kurt's impact still looms so large over music. There are many reasons for the Rock and Roll Hall of Fame to include Nirvana, but the catalog of songs Kurt wrote is central to that recognition. Many bands never even get nominated, but Nirvana were nominated the first year they qualified, and they deserve their place on that hallowed ground.

Kurt has become a touchstone as Nirvana's music continues to find an audience with a new crop of teenagers every year. I think some of his enduring popularity is similar to the way every teen I know ends up reading *The Catcher in the Rye* at some point. Kurt and Nirvana are now part of a rite of passage through adolescence, the true "teen spirit."

I was well past adolescence when Nirvana came on the scene, but their music made me feel young again, alive, full of possibility, and helped me understand some of my own adult angst. The greatest gift Kurt Cobain gave listeners was putting his honest pain into his lyrics. J. D. Salinger did the same thing with his prose in *The Catcher in the Rye*. Both men had demons of different sorts, and they also shared an uncomfortable relationship with fame. And both could proclaim, as Kurt sang on "Serve the Servants" off *In Utero*, "Teenage angst has paid off well."

"Smells Like Teen Spirit" often comes on my car radio, and during those few minutes I'm a teenager again. Suddenly my Volvo wagon—the same car Kurt drove—turns into a hot rod and I'm screaming, "With the lights out, it's less dangerous." The two speeding tickets I've gotten over the past twenty years are solely the fault of Kurt Cobain.

The lyrics to "Smells Like Teen Spirit," Nirvana's biggest hit, were difficult to comprehend and were debated by fans long before the official lyric sheet was finally published. To see how important those lyrics still are, type "s-m-e-l" into Google and you'll see that the most common search in the world for those four letters is " 'Smells Like Teen Spirit' lyrics." Music fans in the UK recently ranked the line "Here we are now, entertain us," as the third-greatest song lyric in music *history*. The *Here We Are Now* book you hold in your hands seeks to reinterpret that lyric into a statement of where *we*, as a collected body of fans, are now after Kurt's death. He's gone, dead for two decades, but here *we* are now. And in that space and time, how do we measure his significance?

Or, in the words of the philosopher, wise man, and sage sometimes known as Larry King, "Why did Kurt Cobain matter?"

ONE

HOLY GRAIL
Music & Influence

Kurt Cobain sold millions of albums, and the most obvious area where his impact can be quantified is in the music industry. During Kurt's lifetime, four official Nirvana albums were released, and since his death there have been six outtake collections or live albums. Most estimates put total sales of those ten releases at somewhere between thirty million and sixty million copies. Sales of *Nevermind* by itself are twenty million worldwide by conservative estimates, and perhaps as high as thirty-five million according to more generous estimates. With those figures, *Nevermind* would rank as the twenty-fifth best-selling album of all time.

Nevermind was a remarkable album by any standard. But while most of the world probably heard the album fully for the first time on compact disc, maybe in their living rooms, I heard it initially in my car on a crappy cassette tape. Furthermore, my cassette was missing the first six seconds of "Smells Like Teen Spirit." My tape started in the middle of Dave Grohl's first drum crash. It was abrupt, but a lot about *Nevermind* was abrupt.

I first heard the album in late August 1991 in the parking lot of the Seattle Tower Records store. It was hot, my windows were down, and I was cranking *Nevermind* loud enough that it drew attention. I didn't want attention. My copy was an illicit bootleg advance that had snuck out the back door, so to speak. I rolled my windows up and sweated in the rare Seattle heat, made steamier by the power of the music.

My copy of the album had come from a friend who worked at Tower, and I had just picked it up before putting it into my car cassette deck. The original source of our leaked copy had dubbed it incorrectly, cutting off the start. All my close friends were music freaks, and we regularly traded with other collectors for live shows, outtakes, and early advance copies. We loved music more than anything in life, and we loved the hunt for unheard tunes, and *Nevermind* was juicy prey. Working in the press, I always got advance copies of albums, and in fact my official advance of *Nevermind* would arrive a week later. But that August, I couldn't wait.

There was much anticipation for *Nevermind.* The band's 1989 debut, *Bleach,* had established Nirvana as a band to watch. *Bleach* had sold around thirty thousand copies, which made it a decent college radio hit, but it wasn't enough to earn the group riches or major fame. But Nirvana's live show had gotten better and better, making them stars in Seattle. Their 1990 "Sliver" single had convinced me that Kurt's songwriting had taken a major leap forward from *Bleach.* When they signed to DGC/Geffen Records in early 1991, it was a huge local story because few Sub Pop bands had made the move up the ladder to a major label. At *The Rocket* we had been touting the Seattle music scene for years, but no local band had broken wide nationally since Heart. Nirvana seemed like our best bet.

When I got the tape back to my office at *The Rocket* I began dubbing cassettes of *Nevermind* for my friends. This was certainly illegal, but I justified that decision knowing that all my friends would buy the album when it officially came out on September 24. That was almost a month away, and it would have been torture to wait. My advance cassette with the clipped "Teen Spirit" spread through Seattle like a fast-moving storm, and by week's end there were hundreds, if not thousands, of dubs.

Sometime around 2004, after Kurt had been dead for a decade, I was with a friend at an open house in Tacoma, thirty miles south of Seattle. The house owner had a homemade cassette of *Nevermind* on the shelf, and it looked like my handwriting on the insert. When the listing agent wasn't looking, I put it into the stereo, hit play, and heard the telltale clipped "Teen Spirit." My early advance tape had flown south.

So much of the story of *Nevermind,* and of Kurt Cobain, has become apocryphal over the years, as his shadow has become bigger than life. Many pundits today suggest they knew in advance that *Nevermind* was going to be a monster hit. But none could have truly predicted the success it had. I certainly didn't have a clue. Listening to it that first time in the parking lot of Tower Records, I loved it, but I thought it too loud, too raw, and too edgy to be a mainstream smash. "Teen Spirit" blew me away, but I couldn't imagine, given where music had been the previous decade, that mainstream radio would play it. To my ears, "Lithium" was the hit on the album, and I thought that "Teen Spirit" would serve only as a kind of advance clarion. I was wrong, of course, but so was DGC/Geffen Records. The label pressed only 46,251 copies of *Nevermind* initially, and that entire first pressing sold out by October. If Geffen had any idea the album was going to be the success it became, they would have made more, since the economy of scale would have lowered their per-disc costs significantly.

A week before *Nevermind* was officially released, a record-release party was held at a Seattle bar. At that party, I put forth the outrageous prediction that the album could sell one hundred thousand copies. That figure was so fantastic, and so outside of what seemed like the realm of possibility at the time, that it earned a quizzical eyebrow raise from Kurt Cobain and the other members of the band. I wasn't the only one forecasting wild success: the guys from Sub Pop Records, who owned a minority interest in *Nevermind,* were touting the same figures. That one-hundred-thousand mark, which was what Sonic Youth's *Goo* had sold in 1990, was considered the upper threshold of the possible for any band playing what we had just begun to call "alternative rock." Though the term "alternative" was loosely applied to any band that didn't fit into mainstream rock—Tom Waits could end up on an alternative radio chart right next to the Cure, though their music had little in common—the name fit for Nirvana, who were certainly not mainstream.

"Smells Like Teen Spirit" changed alternative rock, and changed even the very definition of what mainstream music could encompass. "Teen Spirit" first became an MTV video hit, then a radio smash, and it continued to gain extraordinary momentum. One of Geffen's top executives said that even the label brass were surprised at how fast it climbed the sales charts. All the label had to do, he said, was "get out of the way." The single eventually sold more than a million copies, and that was in a pre-download world where music could only be purchased as a physical item, from a store. On radio, the song topped airplay charts. *Billboard* didn't begin to break down "alternative rock" radio play as a separate category until just after *Nevermind,* but applying their sales-to-airplay chart computation to "Smells Like Teen Spirit" puts that particular song as the most-played alternative rock track ever. Even on mainstream Top 40 radio, where R&B usually dominated, the song went to No. 6.

After that initial pressing of *Nevermind* sold out, it took Geffen time to get more copies printed and delivered to stores. For one of the first times in the modern record business, there was an actual shortage of an album, and *Nevermind* became, for a couple of weeks, impossible to find. The album had debuted at No. 144 on *Billboard*'s chart, so despite its ultimate success, it was not an out-of-the-box smash. The album didn't hit No. 1 on the *Billboard* Hot 200 sales charts for four months. It would ultimately spend 253 consecutive weeks on the charts, though.

Kurt did not immediately become rich off the album. I examined his 1991 federal tax return, and in that year, with a hit album and a sold-out tour, he earned just $29,541, mostly from concert fees. That's evidence of how slow record labels are to pay royalties, but also illustrates how poor Kurt was prior to *Nevermind*'s success. Kurt's paltry income in a banner year also explains why even as a success he was fearful he would be penniless again. He only became rich during the last two years of his life, which is why his fear of scarcity and poverty were ever present. Having been poor for so long, he felt any money he did earn would disappear. Those fears would play a big role in his desire to run away from the world and, ultimately, in his death.

Record sales and airplay are two ways to quantify success in the music business, but those numbers aren't the only measure. Nirvana also changed the music industry because they were an organic runaway success in an era when hit bands were usually heavily shaped, promoted, and marketed by record labels. Before *Nevermind,* it was not uncommon for label brass to pick the songs that would go on a rock album, or to bring in outside musicians to supplement the band in the studio. And while that practice continued in pop, in alternative rock Nirvana, at least temporarily, shifted that. Nirvana's triumph transferred power from the labels to the individual artists, who in the post-Nirvana era had more creative control (for the most part, within rock music). Because of Nirvana, the industry had to rethink where the next rock stars might come from. Labels began to look for talent outside of New York and Los Angeles. Kurt Cobain's success was a breakthrough for bands in Portland, Chapel Hill, Omaha, and countless other places that had been off the radar of the industry. The underdogs were now running the show.

Brian Eno is often credited with saying that the first Velvet Underground album sold only ten thousand copies, "but everyone who bought it formed a band." Listening to rock radio now, two decades after Kurt's death, it sometimes feels as if Eno's paradigm could be far truer for million-copy-selling Nirvana, who possibly spawned a million bands. A wide array of acts, famous and unknown, bring the sound of Nirvana to mind, or at the very least their use of loud/soft dynamics within one song. Major-label bands who it could be argued were influenced by Nirvana include Bush, Weezer, Stone Temple Pilots, Green Day, Feeder, Blink 182, Matchbox 20, Linkin Park, Creed, the White Stripes, Three Days Grace, Puddle of Mudd, Cage the Elephant, Rise Against, A Perfect Circle, Thirty Seconds to Mars, OK Go, System of a Down, Nickelback, Muse, Evanescence, Jet, Three Doors Down, Fuel, Breaking Benjamin, and, of course, Dave Grohl's own Foo Fighters. And these are just the obvious ones, leaving out the hundreds of bands with an obvious Nirvana influence successful enough to have landed record deals, but who aren't as known.

Nevermind transformed rock radio entirely, often making the alternative station the highest rated in a given market. In Los Angeles that was KROQ; in Seattle KNDD; in Atlanta 99X; and in Boston there were two alternative powerhouses, WFNX and WBCN, both of which played Nirvana what seemed like hourly. "Kurt had, and has, the single biggest influence on alternative rock, and certainly on alternative rock radio, of any artist of the past two decades," Marco Collins told me. Collins should know: as a DJ at Seattle station KNDD, he was one of the first to champion "Teen Spirit," helping break the song. "Alternative radio grew to become an actual format because of Kurt's influence. Many of the younger bands getting airplay today went to the school of Kurt and Nirvana. You almost can't overstate his influence. It is, in many ways, even bigger today than it was in the fall of 1991. That sound is everywhere."

To understand *Nevermind*'s impact, and Kurt's, you have to first remember what music was popular in the decade prior. Rock in the eighties had gone in a highly formulaic direction, dominated by soft rock ballads in which style was often put before substance. Almost every hit eighties song was about girls, cars, romance, heartbreak, and partying. Among the top ten singles of that decade were "Physical" by Olivia Newton-John, "Call Me" by Blondie, "Lady" by Kenny Rogers, "Centerfold" by the J. Geils Band, "Flashdance" by Irene Cara, "Endless Love" by Diana Ross, and "Eye of the Tiger" by Survivor. Those well-known chestnuts now sound like they came from an entirely different planet than "Teen Spirit."

Even looking just at the rock genre, the field was dominated by "soft" metal bands who topped the radio charts and MTV play lists from the eighties through the early nineties. Poison, Bon Jovi, Mötley Crüe, Winger, Loverboy, Twisted

Sister, Guns N' Roses, and Van Halen all could "rock," and consistently filled arenas with screaming teenage girls, but they often scored their biggest hits with ballads made into sexed-up videos. They were called "hair bands" because of their giant hairstyles, generally far bigger than the scope of their talent or critical success. Their videos became more important than their songs. Mainstream rock music was so bad in the eighties and early nineties, and so driven by image over substance, that Nirvana enjoyed what was fortuitous timing: they had something to rebel against.

Nirvana recorded *Nevermind* at Sound City Studios in Van Nuys, California, in the spring of 1991, and the band that preceded them in the studio, with a couple days' overlap mixing in a smaller room, was perhaps the most maligned hair-metal band of all, Warrant. Warrant were best known for their cheesy, highly sexualized "Cherry Pie" video, which dominated MTV for a few months in 1990. Kurt grabbed the studio's in-house address system during the days the bands overlapped and belted that song's chorus over the studio's speakers: "She's my cherry pie!" While he was poking fun, Kurt was also putting Warrant on notice that music was shifting. *Rolling Stone* once declared that "Smells Like Teen Spirit" managed a nearly impossible task and "wiped the lingering jive of the Eighties off the pop map overnight." It was hello Nirvana, good-bye Warrant.

Even to those who weren't fans of Nirvana, one aspect of Kurt's impact is simply that his band shifted entirely what music was on the radio or on MTV. "For those turned off by the saccharine pop and hair-metal excess topping the music charts, 'Teen Spirit' was a godsend," Jacob McMurray of Seattle's Experience Music Project museum told me. "Kurt's primal screams, nonlinear prose, and general disdain for the 'meaning' behind his lyrics mirrored an angst-driven push-back." Kurt changed the sound—and the culture—of music.

There was still manufactured pop music after Nirvana, but when Kurt sang about angst and anger, with lyrics that included "an albino, a mosquito, my libido," he changed preconceptions about what topics a song on the radio could cover. A wider—and darker—emotional spectrum opened. Sonically, musical styles that had previously been found only in punk rock, at rock's fringes, became the dominant force. Much has been made about how Nirvana took punk rock to the masses, but Krist Novoselic told me in 1999 that that's not exactly what happened. "We didn't bring punk to the main-stream," Krist said, "we brought the mainstream to punk." Nirvana was not just a flash-in-the-pan band with one hit song that crossed over. Instead, the influence of the band was so great, they opened the minds and ears of the unexpected fan, and indeed the masses.

By the mid-nineties, even Warrant had shifted their music to try to sound like Nirvana.

Legacies in music are preserved not just by sales charts or radio plays but also by articles, essays, and endless lists of the "best" music compiled by critics for magazines, television shows, and websites. Within rock 'n' roll, that critical zeitgeist plays an oversize role in how a band stands in history. For example, take Big Star, who never were commercially successful, but whose critical reputation kept them touring, their albums in print, and in 2013 spawned a documentary film. Usually critics' darlings never sell well, but Nirvana are the rare case of a band that enjoyed high standing with critics *and* simultaneous runaway commercial success.

Nirvana, Kurt Cobain, and usually *Nevermind* appear on the upper reaches of virtually every critic's best-of list of the past twenty years. Both *Spin* and *Rolling Stone* named *Nevermind* the top album of the nineties. A 2000 list compiled by *Rolling Stone* and MTV of the one hundred best pop songs of all time ranked "Smells Like Teen Spirit" third, behind "Yesterday" by the Beatles and "(I Can't Get No) Satisfaction" by the Rolling Stones. In *Rolling Stone*'s 2004 list of the "500 Greatest Songs of All Time," with a slightly different set of voting critics than in 2000, "Smells Like Teen Spirit" came in ninth, and it was the only song in the top ten that came out after 1971.

Critics and fans in the United Kingdom have always held Kurt in even higher esteem. "Smells Like Teen Spirit" was picked by Q magazine's contributors as the third-best song of all time, behind only U2's "One" and Aretha Franklin's "I Say a Little Prayer" (and, surprisingly, ahead of the Beatles' "A Day in the Life," the usual UK top choice). In 2002, *New Musical Express* ranked "Smells Like Teen Spirit" the second-greatest song ever, after only Joy Division's "Love Will Tear Us Apart." The video to "Teen Spirit" almost always shows up in the upper reaches of any critic's list, and it was VH1's pick for the best video of the nineties. *Nevermind* gets the love from not just music magazines: *Entertainment Weekly* named the album the tenth best of all time in 2013.

These accolades go on and on, and they put Kurt and Nirvana in rarefied air. And as time goes by, the band's standing doesn't diminish, which is often the case as new talent and fresh recordings dilute the potential pool of great albums.

Nevermind now competes with not just albums by the Beatles and Led Zeppelin, but also Adele. In several more recent polls, Nirvana have ranked higher than they did a decade ago, and significantly higher than when *Nevermind* came out in 1991.

When *Nevermind* was first released, it earned mixed reviews. Most of them were positive, but only a few were raves. *The Rocket* published one of those raves, calling the album "the kind of music that you fell in love with." The *Boston Globe* review was on the other end of the spectrum, criticizing it as "generic pop-punk that's been done better by countless acts," with lyrics that were "moronic ramblings by singer-lyricist Cobain, who has an idiotic tendency to sound like the Rod McKuen of hard rock." *Rolling Stone*'s review, written by former *Trouser Press* editor Ira Robbins, was favorable but far from glowing. "*Nevermind* boasts an adrenalized pop heart and incomparably superior material [to *Bleach*]," Robbins wrote.

Rolling Stone gave *Nevermind* only three out of five stars, which translates in their rating guide to an "average" album. The review section editor assigns star ratings in *Rolling Stone,* with input from the writer. In a bit of revisionist history, the magazine has since reassigned *Nevermind* a four-star rating in its archived online copy of that original review. In other words, the same album with the same review was later assigned another star by the editors. That's the equivalent of the Michelin Guide changing the historical star rating of a restaurant from two to three stars, not for the current food but retroactively for a course served twenty years prior.

Music critics and editors, like baseball umpires, are known to blow a call (this writer included). But *Nevermind*'s critical rise has gone well beyond that one additional star. In 2003 *Rolling Stone*'s critics and editors ranked it as the seventeenth-greatest album "of all time," ahead of anything by Led Zeppelin, Chuck Berry, Van Morrison, Bruce Springsteen, U2, Stevie Wonder, Fleetwood Mac, the Who, or James Brown. The CD of *Nevermind* that was reviewed in 1991 plays the same music as it did in 2003, and it plays the same music today (though the 2011 reissue has slightly improved sound quality due to remastering). The music on the album didn't change, but in the passing years it somehow got better, or at least the perception of the music shifted, and the importance of the record looms larger.

And *Rolling Stone*'s poll is just one of many where *Nevermind* has improved with age. *Spin* magazine's 1991 year-end list had Teenage Fanclub's *Bandwagonesque* as the top album, R.E.M.'s *Out of Time* as second, and *Nevermind* third. Nine years later *Spin* would name *Nevermind* the best album of the decade. *Rolling Stone*'s 1991 year-end list also rated *Nevermind* third, after R.E.M. and U2.

Those jumps—from being a three-star album upon release, to the third best at the end of 1991, to a four-star album online by the late nineties, to the best of the decade by 1999, before vaulting to seventh-best album of *all time* a dozen years after it was first released—are the absolute proof of Kurt Cobain's enduring legacy. Those leaps in critical standings also prove that Kurt's artistic work grew in perceived significance after his death, even as the music itself didn't change. Some of that is common in rock 'n' roll and happened as well to some rock stars who died young—including Jimi Hendrix, Janis Joplin, and even, recently, Amy Winehouse. Their short lives magnified their relatively small bodies of work, and they are revered in death beyond their fame in life. But even those music legends—all but Winehouse are now in the Rock and Roll Hall of Fame—didn't enjoy the rise in reputation Kurt has experienced. Part of that is simply where Kurt appears on the continuum of rock. Kurt *followed* Jimi Hendrix, and thus Hendrix had to, at least posthumously, compete with Kurt, just as *Nevermind* now competes with Adele's *21,* in critic poll lists. There have been talented rock stars in the last twenty years, including Adele, but so far, in my opinion, none of them would win a critical cage match with Kurt if you compared their full catalog of songs. So he sits at the end of the line, for the moment.

At *The Rocket,* we too did an All Time Greatest Albums list in 1995. *Nevermind* topped that poll as well. I wrote the little piece that talked about the impact of that album back then, just a few years after it had come out. I wrote, "Though we've only had this in our lives for four short years, it has aged well. I can't imagine a time when this pure vision won't rock."

We set the article in the same font as Nirvana's logo, and, of course, it came from the same typesetting machine. Only a graphic designer with a good eye would have noticed, or cared.

The critical standing of any piece of artistic creation rarely remains static, and Kurt's rise over the past two decades has several factors. One is the sad truth that he is dead, so no more Nirvana music is forthcoming. I've heard a lot of what is in the vaults, though not all of it. There are a few little gems here and there, and some interesting Kurt solo jams, but there is no fully conceived masterpiece I'm privy to. The rehearsal tapes are fascinating, though, and I'm sure one day there will be an album just of those recordings. Kurt's songs usually came together in little snippets, with a lyric yelled over a rehearsal, or a melody worked out in a rehearsal jam. But that work in process didn't always yield a finished, finely honed song. "You Know You're Right," which came out on the *Nirvana* album in 2002, is the only posthumous band song I heard in the vaults that I'd rank as great. The 2013 *In Utero* box had a dozen outtakes and rehearsals, but the quality of that material didn't rank with Kurt's best work, at least to my ears. There are Kurt solo songs in the vaults, and some of that will also one day probably appear on an album, but there is no full-band Nirvana Holy Grail recording waiting to be released that I know of.

Without the possibility of another "lost album," the albums that exist now become more important. The Nirvana catalog is also permanently frozen at three studio albums during Kurt's lifetime. The compact nature of that shelf magnifies the importance of what the shelf contains. It makes *Nevermind* a much more significant album than if Kurt had lived as long as Neil Young has, for example, and had produced dozens of albums. Geffen Records, Neil Young's (and Nirvana's) label, ended up suing Neil over his *Trans* album because they felt it was intentionally bad (their legal filing said Neil was "unrepresentative of himself"). Kurt never got the chance to have a midlife musical crisis, which many would argue is what was happening with Neil Young in the mid-eighties. That would surely have been interesting to watch, but the upside is that the three albums he supervised and crafted are what will forever be used to judge his musical legacy. And they are gems.

Kurt's premature death meant the end of Nirvana; the band never considered re-forming with a different singer. It was grief that the fans were left with, and grief that afflicted the band members, too, who felt they had more to say. Dave Grohl told *Mojo* recently, about *In Utero,* "overall it kinda breaks my heart that [it] was the last album we made, because I think there were more [albums] in us." I think Nirvana had more albums in them as well, but we lost those when we lost Kurt.

Critics, music buyers, and musicians don't operate in a vacuum. Success begets success, and some of *Nevermind*'s rise in reputation comes from what neurobiologists call "the winner effect," which is the reward that comes from making a selection you already think will satisfy you, or that your friends have said satisfied them. *Nevermind* built upon itself with record buyers. At the end of the calendar year 1991, *Nevermind* had sold several hundred thousand copies, but by the end of 1992 it had sold several million. It would keep selling millions over the next several years. The album stayed on the *Billboard* charts for a full five years.

Kurt had no idea that *Nevermind* would sell as well as it did, but he did understand the concept that if you reached a certain level of saturation with press, radio, and video, a monster hit could be had. His original title for *Nevermind* was *Sheep,* a term he was sarcastically applying to the American consumer. Would so many "sheep" have bought the album if it were titled *Sheep*? Probably not, but one element of *Nevermind*'s success was both its catchy title and striking cover. The nude baby provoked just enough controversy to get the album stickered in some uptight chains, but not enough to get it banned. Nirvana's label mates on Sub Pop, Tad, also had several controversial album cover choices, but their career was damaged by three different record sleeves that had issues that affected their distribution (controversy is one thing, but if your album is completely unavailable for a time, it dampens sales). Kurt thought about doing something as outrageous as doctoring Pepsi's logo (as Tad had done), but he was far too practical to put his future at risk.

"The winner effect" doesn't usually apply with rock critics, who pride themselves on their contrarian views in print and online. Critical thought usually moves counter to commercial sales. *Nevermind* was not initially an album championed by the press the way, say, the works of Arcade Fire have been; the album's critical weight grew over time. Often when an album rises to the top of the charts without being selected first by critics, the critics will try to take its reputation down because they can't claim ownership of that success. But Nirvana never suffered a significant critical backlash. The band's standing with critics today is near perfect. The catalog is considered nearly flawless.

None of this discourse even brings up the point that *Nevermind*, the seventh-greatest album of all time according to *Rolling Stone,* isn't even Nirvana's best, in my opinion: *In Utero* is. That's what both Krist Novoselic and Dave Grohl also told me over the years, and it's what Kurt said in interviews. But success in the commercial marketplace also plays a role in how an album is remembered, and *In Utero* sold a tenth the number of copies as *Nevermind.* As Nirvana's breakthrough and most successful album, *Nevermind* is always going to be their classic. Still, if I could take only one Nirvana album to a desert island, it would be *In Utero.* Kurt's songwriting had improved, his lyric focus was razor sharp ("Teenage angst has paid off well"), and most of the songs were about his own internal process, which made them deep. I would rank "Heart-Shaped Box," "All Apologies," "Serve the Servants," and "Rape Me" as some of Kurt's most significant lyrics. The music was equally dazzling. His hooks in the choruses were brilliantly conceived. Still, even the remastered *In Utero* in 2013 failed to gain the same critical attention, or sales, as the *Nevermind* reissue.

There is one other explanation for the enduring status of *Nevermind* with critics and fans. This final theory fits neatly into Occam's razor, which is the scientific principle that the simplest answer to any question is most likely the correct one.

Applying Occam's razor to *Nevermind*'s place in history would work like this: *Nevermind* is consistently ranked among the greatest albums of all time because it is.

Nirvana remains an influence on all subsections of rock, from alternative to metal, but Kurt Cobain, bizarrely, also shows up frequently in modern hip-hop. It is one of the oddest elements of his legacy, but one that also shows how wide his cultural swath has been in arenas outside the genre of music he worked in. In the summer of 2013, Jay-Z sampled some of "Teen Spirit" for his hit song "Holy Grail." The first verse ends with

Jay-Z rapping, "I know nobody to blame, Kurt Cobain, I did it to myself." The chorus, sung by superstar Justin Timberlake, also includes lyrics adapted from "Teen Spirit": "We're stupid and contagious, and we all just entertainers."

It was interesting to see two of the biggest stars of music in the 2000s, Jay-Z and Timberlake, sing about Kurt, but the social-media response showed another aspect of Kurt's impact. All over the Internet, the idea of Jay-Z summoning Kurt was called "sacrilegious" and "beyond triple corny," as one Twitter commentator wrote. Those types of remarks come up often whenever Kurt's name or likeness is used outside of Nirvana's music. It suggests that with many people Kurt has more sanctity, or punk authenticity, than other musicians.

"Holy Grail" also caused some observers to revisit the themes of "Smells Like Teen Spirit" all these years later, and whether Kurt should be co-opted. Jay-Z "got the sentiment entirely backwards," *LA Weekly* and *Village Voice* hip-hop critic Chaz Kangas wrote. "'Smells Like Teen Spirit' decried—or at the very least mocked—corporate intrusions into youth culture, and to make it part of an album released as a promotional tie-in for a phone company (strictly for the artist's profit) is dopey at best." Samsung had purchased a million copies of Jay-Z's *Holy Grail* album and gave them away with phones, meaning, in a roundabout way, that the lyric to "Teen Spirit," as sung by Justin Timberlake, became part of the premium for buying a new phone.

But Kangas pointed out to me that Jay-Z's song is just one of at least a dozen times "Teen Spirit" has shown up in hiphop or dance music, used by well-known bands (the Prodigy; Tony! Toni! Toné; Timbaland), and obscure ones (Texas MC Trae tha Truth, DJ Balloon, Credit to the Nation). Kangas says it was a full decade after Kurt's death before he became "the archetype" that hip-hop acts turned to when they wanted to reference rock or a white rock star. One example was when rapper David Banner had a meltdown during a New York showcase and ripped down his own posters around the stage as "Teen Spirit" was played. Banner made devil horns with his fingers and screamed "Rock." The hiphop-loving crowd went crazy. "I think his message was that major labels make so much money off hip-hop, but you have to channel a rock artist to get their respect," Kangas says. "But the fact that he chose to go with 'Smells Like Teen Spirit' as his way of making an 'anti-marketing' effort says much about that song's stature."

Banner played the song frequently during his 2008 tour. When he performed it at a concert at Seattle's Showbox Theater, the crowd went bananas. I think it wasn't simply "Teen Spirit"—which is played regularly at sports events to rile up the crowd—that made the Seattle hip-hop audience go nuts, but instead its contextualization: the very idea that Seattle's most famous song had a place at a hip-hop show.

And if Kurt Cobain is cool within the confines of hip-hop, then the mostly white crowd knew they were cool, too.

It isn't just "Teen Spirit" that hip-hop has embraced; many songs in Nirvana's catalog show up in hip-hop as musical riffs and samples, or as lyrical nods. Some of the best Nirvana samples include Kurt's guitar riff from "Heart-Shaped Box" (3MG), the chorus of "Lithium" (Slug), and even a sample of Kurt's guitar in a cover of the Meat Puppets' "Plateau" (Plan B). The obscure Nirvana track "Moist Vagina" was sampled by Yelawolf, one of Eminem's protégés. The website Whosampled.com lists fifty-five different songs by hip-hop acts that have sampled Nirvana. *Flavorwire* recently ran a story titled "Why is Hip-Hop (and the Rest of Pop Culture) Still So Obsessed with Kurt Cobain?" The answer, writer Tom Hawking suggested, was in part that Kurt died young and is seen as a martyr in the hip-hop community. In a culture where premature, violent death is a dominant theme, Kurt fits in thematically.

Kurt, as a historical figure, also often appears in hip-hop lyrics. His name is evoked to reference suicide or violence. The Game sang "take me away, like a bullet from Kurt Cobain." In 1994, 2Pac rapped about a choice to "blow my brains out like Kurt Cobain." Xzibit rapped, "I lent my shotgun to Kurt Cobain, and the motherfucker never brought it back." DJ Kay Slay rapped, "They want my name next to Kurt Cobain, but I don't sniff cocaine." There are dozens more examples of this motif, including the enduring image Vinnie Paz rapped in "When You Need Me": "My death wish is to die on the Soul Plane, next to Chuck D., Coltrane, and Cobain."

Hip-hop is a music form that makes use of real-life headlines, so Kurt's appearance isn't surprising, even if its frequency is. Some of Kurt's continuing appeal comes from demographics: hip-hop acts skew young, with most artists under forty. Kurt was a major historical figure in these musicians' childhoods, even if Nirvana's music has little externally to do with hip-hop. (Kurt did own Public Enemy's *It Takes a Nation of Millions to Hold Us Back,* his only hip-hop record but a cornerstone of the genre.) Yet Kurt remains an influence on young hip-hop singers. Kangas points out that the pivotal year wasn't as much 1991 as it was 1999: "There were so many recap shows on music television counting down the 'best of the nineties,' and Nirvana topped all those lists, and hip-hop acts saw that, and Kurt became so ubiquitous you can't help but know him." Once everyone knew Kurt's name, his insertion into the music of the moment, which happened to be hip-hop, was inevitable.

There is at least one great truth here that many young hip-hop artists, children in 1991, will miss. But it is a fact not lost on forty-four-year-old Jay-Z. Hip-hop's first foray into the mainstream sales charts began in the eighties, just prior to Nirvana's ascension, and Kurt, for a moment, overshadowed every other music form. "It was weird because hip-hop was becoming this force, then Grunge music stopped it for one second, ya know?" Jay-Z told Pharrell Williams in his 2012 book *Pharrell: Places and Spaces I've Been*. "Those 'hair bands' were too easy for us to take out; when Kurt Cobain came with that statement it was like, 'We gotta wait awhile.'"

TWO

LAMESTAIN ON MY WACK SLACKS
Grunge & Culture

As 1992 started, *Nevermind* became the best-selling album in the United States, knocking Michael Jackson out of the No. 1 slot on the *Billboard* charts. But during much of 1992, as the album continued to sell, Kurt essentially went missing. Courtney was pregnant (she had Frances that August), and Kurt was descending into drug addiction at exactly the same moment he was becoming the biggest star in the world. Nirvana played only a few tour dates during 1992, their biggest commercial year in terms of album sales.

But even Kurt's disappearing act couldn't stop the cultural shift *Nevermind* had wrought. As the Seattle music scene continued to gain worldwide attention and other Seattle bands followed Nirvana to the top of the charts, 1992 became the Year of Grunge. Grunge was a media-created label that had both everything to do with Kurt—it wouldn't have existed without him, or without *Nevermind*'s success—and at the same time almost nothing to do with him.

If the image of Kurt in the "Smells Like Teen Spirit" video clip, with hair in his face and a striped T-shirt on, had been the indelible vision of 1991 on MTV, 1992 looked like a rocker in cutoff jean shorts, a flannel shirt, and a pair of Doc Martens. This is exactly the outfit that actor Matt Dillon wears in Cameron Crowe's movie *Singles,* which came out in 1992. The film was a worldwide success, spawned a hit soundtrack album, and forever wedded Seattle to Grunge.

Singles detailed the lives of a handful of Seattle twenty-somethings as they found romance, started bands, and generally walked about the rainy city making pithy observations. The film had been completed in 1991, but the studio sat on it for a while. When *Nevermind* became a hit, it was quickly released, and wisely marketed as if it were a new Seattle band. And in a way it was: former music journalist Crowe had the prescience to include cameos by a handful of musicians—including Soundgarden's Chris Cornell and Pearl Jam's Eddie

Vedder. By the time the movie came out, they had become major stars. In one scene in the film, a group of these musicians sit around reading a copy of *The Rocket*. At the request of the filmmakers, we had mocked up a fake copy for the film, and the fake band (Eddie Vedder, Jeff Ament, Stone Gossard, and actor Matt Dillon) sat around doing what they did in real life, reading *The Rocket* to see their reviews. After reading the fake review, Eddie Vedder tells Matt Dillon, "A compliment for us is a compliment for you." This was not acting.

It was odd seeing a copy of my magazine in a film, but it was even odder to watch how much impact *Singles* had on how outsiders perceived Seattle. The cutoff-jeans outfit that Matt Dillon wore in the film became what many thought of as the de facto uniform of Seattle music. These were not Kurt Cobain's clothes, or his look, but Kurt got stuck with the image nonetheless. One of the oddest things about *Singles* is that Nirvana isn't on the soundtrack, or in the movie, and yet Nirvana, and Kurt, are forever linked to it in public perception. In 1992, a Montreal television reporter asked the three members of Nirvana why they didn't appear in *Singles*. "Are you part of it at all?" the reporter asked. "Definitely not," Kurt said emphatically. Later in that same interview, Krist

Novoselic said they weren't asked to participate, but Kurt corrected him, saying they were solicited but he wanted no part of *Singles*. "I said 'no,' before even asking you guys," Kurt told his bandmates. "That's because I'm the leader of the band."

By 1992, Kurt, the leader of Nirvana, could say "no," but he and his band were still going to be part of *Singles* in the public's perception, whether they were in the film or not. The phenomenon of Grunge had become a monster that overtook everything in its path, including Kurt Cobain. It could not be corralled.

The word "grunge" first appeared in *The Rocket* in the late eighties as an adjective to describe a certain sonic musical style, a raw and unpolished sound, with distortion, but usually without any other added studio audio effects. Grunge, precapitalization, was almost always applied to a Sub Pop band, and almost always applied to a band produced by Jack Endino. In that context, it meant a mix of garage rock and sloweddown punk. Sub Pop did most of their albums at a low-rent studio named Reciprocal. That studio's acoustics, combined with Endino's production aesthetics, created true capital-G Grunge albums by bands like Mudhoney, Tad, Blood Circus, and a dozen other groups who have now been lost to history. While I'd classify some of Nirvana's early tracks as Grunge, their music always had more pop elements than, say, the output of Mudhoney, who were absolutely a band that played Grunge. In my music-critic hair-splitting, the term didn't really fit most of Nirvana's music, or Kurt's Beatles-influenced melodies. Nirvana's Krist Novoselic also doesn't believe that Grunge, adjective or noun, fits much of Nirvana: he once told me that "School," off *Bleach,* was their Grunge moment. "Kurt bought that riff in," Novoselic told me, "and I said, Oh my God, that is the most Seattle fucking riff I'd heard in my life . . . *That* was the quintessential Grunge song."

The word "Grunge," as an adjective and not a noun, had been kicked around in rock 'n' roll for decades before it came to describe a generation. Lester Bangs used it in an October 1972 record review of a metal band in *Creem.* Before that, it appeared in liner notes to a reissue of a 1957 Johnny Burnette Trio album, where the rockabilly guitar playing was described as "grungy." Mark Arm of Mudhoney is often credited with coining the term, but he says he heard it from friends in Australia where edgy singer-songwriter Tex Perkins was dubbed "the high priest of grunge." The first print use of "Grunge" in the Northwest can be traced to a letter to the editor by Mark

Arm that appeared in the Seattle fanzine *Desperate Times* in 1981. In it, Arm complained about the band Mr. Epp and the Calculations: "Pure grunge! Pure noise! Pure shit!" Arm just so happened to be the lead singer for Mr. Epp.

Sub Pop Records first used the word in promotional materials describing Green River, a group that included Arm— plus Jeff Ament and Stone Gossard, who later formed Pearl Jam. "Ultra-loose GRUNGE that destroyed the morals of a generation," the release read.

That Green River record was produced by Jack Endino, who could have trademarked the Grunge sound as well as the name. Kurt hired Endino to produce early demos in 1988. The result of that first demo tape, and a few other lucky breaks, caused Sub Pop to sign Nirvana. With that deal in hand, Nirvana recorded their debut, *Bleach,* at Reciprocal, with Endino producing. Most of that album would qualify as Grunge, yet "About a Girl" was "pure pop," in Endino's words. Kurt told Endino he had listened to *Meet the Beatles* for three hours straight before writing that song.

The sessions for the entire *Bleach* album cost just $600, an indication of both how basic the studio was and Endino's low rates. Sub Pop was so poor they couldn't front that small sum, and Kurt didn't have it either, of course. Kurt had to borrow the money to pay the studio from Jason Everman, who played bass in Nirvana briefly. Everman told me Kurt never paid him back. But *Bleach* would earn Nirvana mostly positive reviews and garner them airplay on college radio stations. It was a start.

By 1989, Sub Pop bands were generating a lot of attention in Europe, and specifically in the UK. There were several competing weekly music publications in England that were always searching for the next big thing, and it was there where "grunge" became a term to describe a movement, instead of one style of music. In a British newspaper, Mark Arm described the streets of Seattle being "paved with grunge." Almost overnight, "grunge" became "Grunge," as the British music press began using the name in headlines. Looking for something to write about now that punk had faded, they grabbed hold of Seattle bands, and "Grunge" appeared in nearly every headline. Mark Arm hated that he'd started the trend, but he couldn't stop it. "It seemed a way to pigeonhole every band from Seattle," Arm said. "These bands didn't sound alike, but suddenly, what had been an adjective became a noun."

The media in the US also needed a way to describe the fashion, music, and lifestyle shifts that were embodied by youth in Seattle, and so "Grunge" made its way back home. As with every cyclical youth-cultural trend—from greasers to hippies to punks—there was a shred of truth to the trend, but also much projection, exaggeration, and amplification in how the press reported it. If the eighties had been an era personified by yuppies, blue-collar no-nonsense Seattle was the antidote. Seattle was a city of bookstores and coffee shops that helped support a lifestyle that was contemplative. All those espresso shops needed baristas—the job Matt Dillon's character had in *Singles*—and those positions were perfect for musicians. Still, the only person I knew in Seattle in 1991 who dressed like Matt Dillon in *Singles* was Pearl Jam's Jeff Ament. That should come as no surprise, as Dillon wore many of Ament's clothes in the movie.

But the media has always fed on trends and movements, and when a handful of Seattle bands gained international attention—and when one of those bands (Nirvana) sold thirty-five million albums—something had to be made of it in the press. As these Grunge "trend" stories began to appear in magazines and newspapers over the world, there was the inevitable backlash in Seattle where many, including Kurt Cobain, felt that a varied and diverse music scene with hundreds of bands had been condensed to one word. Kurt was a good enough music critic—he had once imagined himself as a fanzine editor—to know that there were major differences between the sounds of Nirvana and the more metal-leaning Soundgarden, but both were now classified as Grunge. In nearly every interview Kurt or Nirvana did henceforth with radio or television, they were asked about Grunge. While Kurt was happy to have his music influence other bands, and to also be able to wear a T-shirt adorned with the logo of his favorite indie band when he was on television, he didn't want to be seen as the leader of a youth movement. He usually refused to answer questions about Grunge, or responded with sarcasm. He never specifically addressed why he hated the term so much, but many other Seattle musicians told me why they disliked it—because it diminished their individual artistry and turned their art into a commodified and marketed trend.

Evidence of the Seattle backlash toward the use of the word "Grunge" came with one of the most delicious spoofs ever pulled on a major newspaper. In 1992, New York–based magazines had begun to regularly send writers to Seattle to document "the scene" and capture the essence of Grunge. They would fly into town, hang in local clubs, try to catch the "flavor" of "the scene," and look for juicy quotes. As a result, locals, particularly musicians, became resentful when asked about Grunge by out-of-towners.

Sub Pop was ground zero for anything related to Grunge, at least in the media's mind, and reporters were desperate to try to break a Grunge exclusive. In November 1992, a *New York Times* reporter was assigned to write about "Grunge culture." The writer phoned Sub Pop, and Megan Jasper answered the phone. When the reporter asked her if fans of Grunge had a lingo, Jasper informed him, sarcastically, that there was a secret "Seattle Grunge language." The writer took the bait. On the spot Jasper made up several nonsense sayings, telling the reporter they were Grunge code words known only within Seattle culture.

The list was titled "Grunge Speak" when it was published in *The New York Times* the next day. "Lamestain" was what a Grunge musician would call an "uncool person" and a derogatory term, the *Times* reported. "Wack slacks" was the name for now-fashionable ripped jeans like Kurt's. When rockers in Seattle said they were "swingin' on the flippity-flop," it meant they were hanging out. "Bound-and-hagged" was staying home on a weekend night. What made "Grunge Speak" even more strange was that in the same article, Sub

Pop's Jonathan Poneman was quoted on how people in Seattle resented the intrusion of media attention: "All things Grunge are treated with the utmost cynicism and amusement . . . because the whole thing is a fabricated movement, and always has been," he said.

Seattle howled at the "Grunge Speak" piece, including Kurt Cobain. This was truly the funniest thing that had ever happened in the Seattle music scene, but it also illustrated the insanity of the phenomenon of Grunge. Seattle was being treated as if it were some newly discovered tribe, with its own customs, dress, and language. *Entertainment Weekly* wrote the next year, in a true moment of hyperbole, "There hasn't been this kind of exploitation of a subculture since the media first discovered hippies in the sixties."

While everyone in Seattle laughed at the *New York Times* story, and we even wrote about it in *The Rocket,* several weeks passed before the rest of the country caught on. Finally, the Chicago magazine *The Baffler* reported that *The New York Times* had been had. Rather than admit they erred, the *Times* declared it was actually *The Baffler* who had been hoaxed, and that the "Grunge Speak" list was real. The *Times* went so far as to demand *The Baffler* apologize. They didn't, of course, but it is worth mentioning that *The New York Times* has never run a correction, and twenty years later "Grunge Speak" is still posted on the newspaper's website without any indication that it's a hoax. Either someone at that paper truly believes that people in Seattle used (or still use) the term "bloated, big bag of bloatation" to describe a drunk, or Grunge is responsible for the longest-running prank ever pulled on *The New York Times*.

Around the time of "Grunge Speak," I hit my own apex of how crazy Grunge had become when another gullible out-of-town reporter phoned *The Rocket*. He was from an eastern Canadian newspaper and claimed a story had just come over the Canadian wire services about how officials were concerned Seattle would be overrun with teenagers. Public-safety leaders, this guy said, were quoted as predicting that a million youth were headed for Seattle, like the influx San Francisco saw during the 1967 Summer of Love. This reporter claimed his wire story said Seattle police had already installed barricades to control crowds. I laughed and told him he'd been had.

But this tenacious reporter wouldn't let go. He kept calling back, thinking he was on to an exclusive, and that I could help him confirm it. He insisted I "look out my window" to make sure this army of flannel-clad teens hadn't already arrived. For a half second I wondered if I was the one getting hoaxed. But things had been so crazy that year, and so beyond what I'd ever imagined, I did look out the window. There was, of course, no mass of teenage runaways filling the streets of Seattle.

If I was living with this kind of nonsense, imagine Kurt, as the supposed "leader" of a nonexistent "movement," and the amount of absurdity he was dealing with. He was pestered by reporters everywhere he went. When he was asked about the "Seattle scene" by a journalist, Kurt said, "All scenes are relevant, but they all phase into nothing, or go away. . . . They are claiming we finally put Seattle on 'the map.' What map?"

That silly Canadian wire-service report about the masses of kids did contain a tiny bit of foreshadowing, however. Out my same window, seven years later, there actually were hordes of kids, thousands instead of millions, fighting police behind barricades. Clouds of tear gas drifted up into my office during one wild week in November 1999. That month Seattle's streets were filled with angry youth for protests that would be known as the Battle in Seattle, the WTO riots.

If during the Summer of Grunge reporters were looking everywhere to land the ultimate Seattle story, Kurt was the biggest game of them all, and they hunted him in every nook of the Pacific Northwest. He wisely chose to spend that summer living in Los Angeles awaiting his daughter Frances's birth and did not return to Seattle until the fall. He couldn't hide completely, however. The September issue of *Vanity Fair* captured both Courtney and Kurt. It was the single most controversial article ever written about them. The headline read: STRANGE LOVE: ARE COURTNEY LOVE, LEAD DIVA OF THE POST-PUNK BAND HOLE, AND HER HUSBAND, NIRVANA HEARTTHROB KURT COBAIN, THE GRUNGE JOHN AND YOKO? OR THE NEXT SID AND NANCY? The story contained allegations of drug use, of Frances being born in poor health, with Courtney described as a "train-wreck personality." When Los Angeles County's child protective services stepped in to threaten to take Frances away, Kurt was beside himself. Just a day after Courtney gave birth, Kurt went to the delivery room with a loaded pistol, intending for the two of them to commit suicide together. He was talked down by Courtney, and Eric Erlandson of Hole helpfully whisked away the gun, but the incident shows how on the edge Kurt was. Guns and suicide were already established parts of his world, even with a one-day-old daughter next to him.

But something also shifted with Kurt in the season of Grunge, and the change ultimately affected his legacy for the better. Kurt had always been liberal, and Nirvana had played several antiwar benefits before they became famous. But by 1992, Kurt was motivated to speak out on social issues he felt important. Perhaps he thought that if he was going to be asked the same questions about Grunge over and over in every interview, he'd better shift the control and use these opportunities to affect change. He chose to discuss feminism, bigotry, racism, and intolerance, topics he spoke about in every interview he did for the rest of his life.

The transformation was, in some ways, remarkable. Kurt Cobain, who previously had spent most of his spare time watching inane television or playing with his Evel Knievel action figures, became the most outspoken man in rock 'n' roll. His pro-feminist stance and his support of gay rights became almost crusades for him at this point. If Grunge gave Kurt a soapbox, he was going to use it for good.

The most obvious example of Kurt's new outspokenness came in his liner notes to the B-side collection *Incesticide,* which was released at the end of 1992. The notes are unlike any other liner notes ever penned by a rock star. They are more of an open letter to fans, and the public, than a description of the music on the album. In them, Kurt urges "homophobes" to no longer buy his albums. He wrote: "If any of you, in any way, hate homosexuals, people of a different color, or women, please do this one favor for us—leave us the fuck alone. Don't come to our shows and don't buy our records."

With this battle cry, Kurt was trying to do something during the mad year of Grunge that was unheard of in the marketplace of pop culture: he was attempting to self-select who bought his records. Nirvana's initial fan base was made of their peers, progressive fans who came out to tiny clubs to watch a band touring in a van. But as *Nevermind* broke massive, Nirvana no longer had one type of fan. That bothered a control freak like Kurt, particularly as Grunge became a label he was saddled with, and particularly when Nirvana's audiences began to grow.

And when his music was co-opted, Kurt became enraged. In those same liner notes Kurt wrote about a real-life incident of two men in Reno raping a girl while they sang lyrics to the song "Polly" from *Nevermind*. Kurt said they were "two wastes of sperm and eggs." Hinting at his own suicide, or at least retirement, he added, "I have a hard time carrying on knowing there are plankton like that in our audience." Kurt was particularly upset that "Polly," a song he wrote about a newspaper account he'd read of the torture and rape of a fourteen-year-old girl, would then later be used as a soundtrack to another horrific crime. The song had displayed his extraordinary creative mind, written from the view of the attacker in the deplorable crime, but it was set into a catchy pop song. Oddly, Kurt wrote three separate songs over the course of his career about rape, one on every album Nirvana put out: "Floyd the Barber," "Polly," and, obviously, "Rape Me."

After Kurt wrote "Rape Me," he felt he had to explain himself to the media. He told *Spin,* "It's like she's saying, 'Rape me, go ahead, rape me, beat me. You'll never kill me. I'll survive this and I'm gonna fucking rape you one of these days, and you won't even know it.'" In the same interview Kurt said he hoped *In Utero* would shift some of rock's "misogyny." "Maybe it will inspire women to pick up guitars, and start bands—because it's the only future of rock 'n' roll."

Rape became just one of many social issues Kurt often spoke out against, and Nirvana performed several benefit concerts for anti-rape groups. They also played benefits for anti-hate groups, against racism, and for gay rights. The more mainstream Kurt's music became and the more *Nevermind* sold, the more he felt the need to try to control his agenda. Nirvana played mostly loud, raucous guitar rock, and that style of music—be it Grunge or heavy metal—primarily attracted a young male demographic that oftentimes felt concerts were a place to work off aggression or party. That stereotype had fit Kurt at one point in his youth, but once he saw his own countenance reflected back at him from his concert crowds, he tried to shift that vibe. He tried to pick bands who were less mainstream to open concerts for Nirvana. Mirroring his comments on women being the future, he also gave opportunities to female-fronted bands like L7 and Shonen Knife.

In some ways, Kurt was successful in gaining back some control. Grunge became a much more finely nuanced musical movement than heavy metal, and there were opportunities for females that hadn't really existed within hard rock before. Courtney's band, Hole, inspired a generation of young women as well, and so did Babes in Toyland, the Breeders, Veruca Salt, and Seattle's own Seven Year Bitch.

Kurt promoted these groups whenever he did an interview and wore T-shirts with their names on them, and that was one of the reasons he was often cited as being a feminist. He was comfortable with that title, and both he and Courtney used it to describe him. "No one ever talks about how many of these rock guys were just sexist, asshole jocks who used alternative rock to maintain the same misogynistic power they had in high school," Courtney Love once told me. Kurt, she said, was different. And I think she was right.

Kurt's feminism has inspired several academic studies. Cortney Alexander wrote her master's thesis on gender identity in Grunge, focusing primarily on Kurt. She titled it after one of Kurt's quotes: *"I'm Not Like Them, but I Can Pretend": A Feminist Analysis of Kurt Cobain's Gender Performance.* The blog *Gender Across Borders* has written, "Cobain often identified himself with women, racial and gender minorities because he felt alienated from the cultural expectation of masculinity." The blog *The Individualist Feminist* has a separate page devoted to Kurt. It calls him an "outspoken feminist" and quotes, by chapter and verse, every mention he made that supported women's rights in the press. There were many.

Kurt was not the first—nor would he be the last—rock star to address social issues, but because he had the biggest pulpit in music in the early nineties, his words were heard and had an effect. He had also grown up in an environment where overt homosexuality was not tolerated, and where bias and violence toward sexual minorities were part of the fabric of life. Once he was famous, he often spoke out in support of gay rights. In 1992, he did an extensive interview with *The Advocate* simply because he knew that magazine had an audience of gay readers. Kurt made headlines around the world when he told the magazine he was "gay in spirit" and "probably could be bisexual." He inflated parts of his own childhood history, claiming he was often beaten up around Aberdeen because some thought him gay (none of his friends confirm these beatings, and doubt they happened). Kurt also said he'd been arrested in Aberdeen for spray-painting HOMO SEX RULES on a wall (the police report of this arrest specifies it was actually the nonsensical slogan AIN'T GOT NO HOW WATCHAMACALLIT). His interview with *The Advocate* presented him as pro-gay from a much younger age than when he actually became politically aware. Kurt did this, at least in part, because he very much wanted to be embraced by the gay community, and because he felt a kinship to gays and lesbians as outcasts judged by society, which is how he viewed himself.

The *Advocate* story furthered the perception that Kurt was possibly bisexual (though no evidence of this exists). "His bisexuality caused a lot of discussion, and he made a point of it being public," sexuality expert Dr. Pepper Schwartz told me. "I think the idea of incorporating that into his life, and still being married, made bisexuality seem like another flavor, or, if you will, a choice one could make."

Kurt already had a large gay following, but his comments

further cemented that connection. Kurt was a style icon not just in music but also in fashion—and particularly within gay culture. Several popular websites break down his most famous outfits so they can be emulated and copied exactly. *Out* magazine ran a piece in 2013 titled "Get the Look: Kurt Cobain," which detailed where to shop for clothes to mimic Kurt's look.

It would, oddly, be in fashion that the word "Grunge" would continue to survive in current culture, a life that the word has not had within music. It was the constant need for trend stories that created Grunge in the first place, and by the middle of the nineties, after Kurt's death, that trend was declared dead by the same kingmakers who had flown out to Seattle and looked for patterns in every coffeehouse or concert stage. The Grunge movement, just as Kurt had predicted, had "phase[d] into nothing." The headlines, at least in music, moved on to further stops, with hip-hop culture and electronica.

To many kids in Seattle today, Grunge means their parents' music. It is often, however, thought of fondly and with nostalgia, not unlike how teenagers in the seventies looked back upon the sixties. To teens today, Grunge is a more meaningful era from back when rock music mattered, and when, or so they imagine, every street corner sported a future superstar dressed up just like Matt Dillon in *Singles*.

THREE

THE $6,000 COBAIN TRENCH COAT
Style & Fashion

Of all the aspects of Kurt Cobain's legacy, Kurt himself would be most surprised by his impact on fashion. We know that to be true because by 1992, two years before his death, Kurt was already a fashion icon, and he expressed amazement to friends that a style of dress he had adopted out of practicality had become the stuff of runway shows. It surprised Kurt, but then everything the year after *Nevermind* was head-shaking. Many rock stars have an impact on fashion, but Kurt's influence has truly been a bizarre outgrowth of his fame, and one that will last (even if his music will undoubtedly be his greatest legacy). Kurt very much planned his musical career, writing out imaginary interviews with magazines in his journals long before he became famous. But he never considered that if he became a star, his ripped-up jeans and flannel shirts might one day end up on the runways of New York fashion shows.

Kurt became a fashion icon essentially by accident, but in the fall of 1991 so much of what he did and said had a larger effect on the consumer marketplace than he could have imagined. That irony and power of accidental marketing was never greater than in the case of "Smells Like Teen Spirit." Kurt wrote the song after seeing graffiti written on his bedroom wall by a friend who was taunting Kurt, implying that he had another girl's scent on him. He had no idea when he crafted his lyrics that Teen Spirit was the name brand of a deodorant marketed to teenage girls. It was only after the song was recorded, and on its way to being a monster hit, that he found this out. He was astounded that he'd written a song—one that would go on to become Nirvana's anthem, his own signature piece—without knowing that the title referred to a product. When the song became a hit, sales of Teen Spirit deodorant skyrocketed. The brand, produced by Mennen, added new fragrances to capitalize on the attention. The year after *Nevermind* was released, Colgate-Palmolive bought Mennen for $670 million.

When we address Grunge's impact on the larger fashion

industry, we are actually talking about more than just Kurt, because he wasn't the only style influencer. Instead, fashion's interest in Grunge also was an outgrowth of the impact of the handful of bands and musicians associated with that genre who became, at least for a time, household names. That would include Eddie Vedder, Chris Cornell, and Layne Staley, who were all also trendsetters who saw their styles mimicked widely. But as Kurt was the biggest star of Grunge, and in many ways its unwilling poster boy, his influence is outsize by comparison. At the very least, the impact of Grunge on fashion without Kurt, or without *Nevermind*'s thirty-five million sales, would have been significantly less.

Rock stars have been shaping fashion since the early days of rock 'n' roll. When Elvis slicked back his hair, millions followed suit. The Beatles influenced hairstyles and helped introduce the Nehru jacket to Western culture. In the eighties, hip-hop act Run-DMC wrote a song called "My Adidas," fueling the resurgence in status sneakers. The names of shoe brands pop up regularly in hit songs today, and popular music plays an increasing role as a marketing tool for all apparel.

Kurt Cobain stands out from that pattern because he was an unwilling style role model, and initially an unaware one.

The Beatles knew they were fashion icons, evidenced by their matching and made-to-order costumes for the *Sgt. Pepper's* album art. But Kurt was the unusual fashion magnet whose style was more a reflection of his own laziness than it was an effort to impress. He didn't put on a different set of clothes before he walked onstage; his stage clothes were sometimes the only clothes he had. One of the reasons Kurt became such an icon was *because* he rarely changed his clothes. He cemented a singular look by keeping the same clothes on day in and day out, or at least wearing a very limited array of tattered items. Never in history had a rock star been so consistent with a style. Though he changed his hair in the last year of his life and began to wear sunglasses to hide from admirers, his clothes remained the same for more than a decade.

The term that often comes up when fashion writers talk about the "Grunge look" as "anti-fashion," which is one of the keys to understanding why Grunge style has been so lasting. Since it's a "reactive" style—a rebellion—it comes in and out of favor whenever a designer feels fashion needs a reboot.

Punk rock was also clearly accompanied by a fashion that went in an unusual and unexpected direction, and it preceded Grunge by a full decade. Many of the styles created by British punks eventually found their way onto fashion runways, modified by designers. But with the original punk rockers, their choices—Mohawk haircuts, safety pins through lips, distressed *Wild One* leather jackets—were *conscious* attempts to make a statement. Vivienne Westwood helped create that punk aesthetic, and has explained that punk's goal was "seeing if one could put a spoke in the system."

Kurt Cobain, on the other hand, came to his personal style out of necessity and fell into a fashion-icon role almost entirely by accident. His tousled hairstyle, for example, was due partially to the fact he couldn't afford shampoo, and therefore washed his hair with body soap. In 2003, a hairstyling product line called Bed Head was launched that sought to create, with a twenty-five-dollar shampoo and accompanying products, the same look Kurt achieved with a twenty-nine-cent bar of soap. Kurt essentially rolled out of bed and, moments later, was a style icon.

There were three central factors that influenced what clothes Kurt wore, and that in turn would shape his particular fashion influence: the climate in western Washington, where he lived (wet and cold); his financial situation (dire); and his shame about being thin (large enough that he wore layers of clothes to try to mask his physique). This last factor was the most significant to his clothing choices. Kurt was so skinny that clothes seemed to hang off him, so he wore layer over layer. He was also always cold, so a long woolen coat was not out of the question for him even in summer. For one trip to the beach in 1987 with his then girlfriend Tracy Marander, he wore a pair of thermal long johns, two pairs of Levi's, a long-sleeved shirt, and two sweatshirts. On the warmest day of the year in the Northwest, he might be dressed like he was wintering in Cleveland.

Kurt was also destitute for most of his adult life. A majority of his clothes came from garage sales, thrift shops, or surplus stores. There was one army-navy store in downtown Olympia, Washington, that supplied his thermal long underwear and many of the ten-dollar flannel shirts that would become the stuff of legend. The colors were often dark yellows, light blues, olive greens, and black. These hues would become the color spectrum of Grunge fashion. They were less a conscious plan by Kurt to pick that palette than they were an outgrowth of the fact that these garments had originally been designed as outdoor wear.

When fashion designers began to mimic Kurt in late 1992, it marked a show of Kurt's sway in culture, but it was also a watershed moment in fashion itself: never in the history of fashion had so much money been spent trying to look so

ordinary. Whether Grunge could even be considered a legitimate fashion trend was constantly debated during Kurt's lifetime, and still at times is debated in the fashion press. "Grunge
is nothing more than the way we dress when we have no
money," designer Jean Paul Gaultier said in 1993.

Vogue first celebrated the idea of Grunge fashion with a
December 1992 feature in which skinny models were pictured
in sweaters, flannel shirts, and $600 scarves that were made
to look as if they were from Goodwill. But in an about-face,
Vogue, one of the first magazines to use the word "Grunge" in
reference to fashion, by the end of the nineties called the trend
a "clumpy downtrodden look" and "one of the worst" of all
nineties trends. Like Grunge music, Grunge fashion became a
lightning rod for controversy.

Kurt's emergence as a fashion influencer began as *Nevermind*
flew up the album charts in the fall of 1991 and the "Smells
Like Teen Spirit" video became a hit. Radio and MTV were
primarily responsible for breaking *Nevermind,* not the press.
Consequently, most of the public first saw Kurt, as was the
case with the Beatles, on television. He was tremendously
photogenic on television, where the camera added the ten

pounds he needed. He had that certain star quality that was a combination of attractiveness and mystery, so he looked entrancing in photos. To put it in the words of one writer for *BuzzFeed,* "Kurt Cobain was super hot."

With blond hair, blue eyes, high cheekbones, and a wide mouth, Kurt had movie-star looks without effort or makeup. He was almost impossibly handsome for a rock star, but his long hair and relaxed style of dress underplayed that and made him appear boyish, even at twenty-seven. His hair, which was so light when he was young it was nearly white, made him stand out in an era when most male rock superstars had dark hair. Other than Elvis (born blond, but who dyed his hair black), or Robert Plant, Kurt may be the single most influential natural blond in rock history.

But Kurt's hair didn't stay blond. He was fond of dying it outrageous shades, and with wild shades of dye. He preferred to use Kool-Aid for hair dye, which made for odd colors. It was an unconventionally handsome look he presented, perfect for the style of music he was playing. If he'd arrived to stardom in a suit and with short hair, his looks would have lessened his punk-rock authenticity. Kurt was able to have it both ways: to be a teen idol to women and gay men, but also to be taken seriously as a musician.

The world's crush on Kurt began with the "Smells Like Teen Spirit" video clip. However, the video mostly hid his good looks behind distorted visual effects and smoke and by keeping the camera focused on every point but Kurt's face. But when Nirvana first appeared on *Saturday Night Live* in January 1992, he didn't have that ability to direct the camera angles; his handsomeness couldn't be hidden any longer and a fashion star was born. It was Nirvana's network broadcast debut, and millions tuned in. The clothes Kurt wore that night were probably not a conscious attempt to craft a particular image, but it was a style that nonetheless would prove lasting. He wore a "Flipper" T-shirt, plugging one of his favorite indie bands, and an oversize light-blue cardigan sweater. His jeans were so ripped there was as much skin showing as there was fabric. Under his jeans, Kurt wore long underwear, as per usual. That he had on multiple layers under hot studio lights and did not sweat profusely was remarkable.

His look emphasized his ordinariness, and that was dramatically different from the approach of other bands of the era. A month before Nirvana was on *Saturday Night Live,* the hair-metal darlings of the moment, Skid Row, had been the show's musical guest. Their style—big hair, all black leather—was in dramatic contrast to Kurt's. Two weeks preceding Nirvana's appearance, MC Hammer had been the musical guest, representing another style extreme with his gold chains and parachute pants.

As always, Kurt's wardrobe was so limited that there was constant repetition. He was photographed in his same *Saturday Night Live* outfit often. In the "Teen Spirit" video, he wore roughly the same clothes, though his shirt was brown-and-green striped for that shoot. His clothing choices that fall became what the public would come to think of as the Kurt Cobain uniform, or, in a larger framework, the Grunge look. Rarely did it vary—Kurt complained to a friend, a month after *Nevermind* was released, that he only owned one pair of jeans.

None of this is to suggest that Kurt was oblivious to the fact that image was one of many elements of show business. He wore T-shirts of bands he liked—including Mudhoney, Daniel Johnston, and the Melvins—because he wanted to serve as a human billboard. But he was also often photographed in a long-sleeved shirt featuring the name of the UK music magazine *Sounds*. He had been given the T-shirt for free, which was often the main reason Kurt picked a particular garment.

In the fall of 1991, Kurt began a relationship with Courtney Love, who knew the names of every famous designer in the world. Love, in her own way, had helped launch a trend with the baby doll, or "kinder-whore," look, a mishmash of femininity and grit that has also had a lasting design impact. Sometimes Kurt and Courtney wore the same clothes, with her donning one of his army jackets and him occasionally wearing one of her slips over his clothes. As he became more famous, he tried harder to play against gender roles, wearing a tutu onstage and for photo shoots several times. On a half dozen occasions he wore dresses in concert, again playing off expected gender roles. Unlike his normal style, which he took up for practicality, Kurt's cross-dressing was a very conscious attempt to poke fun at the seriousness of rock archetypes. That trend did not catch on. Kurt was a beautiful man, but— wearing a slip with his skinny arms and four days' stubble on his chin—he did not come off as a glamorous woman.

At the end of 1991, *Sassy* magazine approached Kurt to appear on its cover, and he agreed, with the condition that he must appear with Courtney. The photo session was set for the day following *Saturday Night Live*. For the shoot, the magazine ordered a variety of clothing samples for Kurt to try on, to see what look he felt comfortable with. He rejected them all and said he preferred to wear his own clothes. He showed up wearing the exact same clothes he'd had on television the previous night. Courtney, in contrast, had requested specific labels and high-end designers. "She wanted earrings from Tiffany's, and clothes from Agnès B, and a few others," recalled Andrea Linett, then the fashion editor of *Sassy*. "Courtney was the first time I'd seen anyone in a Grunge band who was really into labels." Linett had thought to bring an old sweater of her father's, and Kurt preferred that to the designer clothes. He wore Linett's father's sweater for some photos (including one that later appeared in *Vanity Fair*), but he wore his own light-blue cardigan sweater for *Sassy*'s cover.

That cover photograph, showing Courtney kissing Kurt, proved to be iconic and is the most famous photo of the two of them together. The clothes Kurt wore that day, particularly his oversize fuzzy cardigan, would have an impact on fashion designers for years. Linett thinks that the styling of that photo shoot was an overlooked key ingredient. "Grunge is not about the design of clothes, but instead the styling approach," she said. With Kurt, that styling meant unkempt, baggy clothing, hair that appeared unwashed even if it was clean, and the intentional juxtaposition of different styles (letter sweaters meet distressed jeans). Linett, who later went on to work in fashion at *Lucky* magazine and then eBay, says the Grunge look continues to affect fashion because it's not about one color or cut of fabric. "My mother could put together an outfit that you'd call Grunge from her closet, if it was styled correctly," she said.

Even in Seattle, some were seduced by the fashion trendiness. That was never clearer to me than at the 1992 Washington State fair. Booths sprang up along the midway, next to the ones that sold sunglasses and corn on the cob, hawking GRUNGE GEAR. Their wares included CDs and T-shirts by the hit bands of the day, but also flannel shirts, ripped-up jeans, and combat boots.

Almost identical flannel shirts could be found at hundreds of surplus or outdoor stores, some just outside the gates of the fair, for half the price of the shirts at the booth. But even in Washington, even a few dozen miles from where Kurt Cobain wrote the songs that made *Nevermind* a hit, vendors had discovered that the word "Grunge" made things sell like hotcakes.

One can easily date the exact moment when Grunge overtook high fashion: November 3, 1992. On that day, designer Marc Jacobs unveiled his Spring 1993 collection for the Perry Ellis line. Jacobs's first model, Christy Turlington, came on the New York catwalk to a barrage of flashbulbs and gaped mouths. She was wearing a black knit skullcap, a sleeveless flannel shirt, a fuzzy sweater similar to what Kurt wore on the cover of *Sassy,* combat boots, and a trench coat. It was, as one headline proclaimed, "The Day That Grunge Became Glam." Later during that same week, Anna Sui debuted her take on Grunge, which included more hippie-ish elements, while hot young designer Christian Frances Roth showed Grunge outfits using leggings and shirts tied around waists, for a more subdued influence.

But it was Jacobs's designs, and his $300 flannel shirt, that got the attention of the mainstream press. Jacobs's "Grunge collection" was discussed on network news broadcasts, in newspaper stories, and in the opening monologue of late-night talk shows. The very idea that "Grunge" could be a term even used in fashion was enough to draw a laugh from many.

Some in the fashion press lauded Jacobs's creativity, but others were apoplectic. James Truman, editor of *Details,* a magazine that would feature Nirvana on the cover in November 1993, was one of the most quoted. "[Grunge is] *un*fashion," Truman said. "Grunge is about *not* making a statement, which is why it's crazy for it to become a fashion statement." Fashion writer Suzy Menkes handed out GRUNGE IS GHASTLY buttons. Fashion critic Bernadine Morris said the

Jacobs collection was "mixing everything up . . . A typical outfit looks as if it were put together with the eyes closed in a very dark room." *Vogue*'s spread on Grunge fashion spurred one reader to write to the editor: "Your rendition of Grunge fashion was completely off. If the whole idea is to dress down, why picture models in $400 dresses? No one who can honestly relate to music labeled Grunge is going to pay $1,400 for a cashmere sweater (especially when they can buy a perfectly comfortable flannel shirt for fifty cents at the local thrift store)."

The controversy grew further when Marc Jacobs admitted he'd never even been to Seattle. Jacobs might have been his own worst enemy with the fashion establishment when he stated in the press that his Grunge collection was "a little fucked up," and admitted he found "a two-dollar flannel shirt on St. Mark's Place" and had sent it to Italy to be copied in $300-a-yard plaid silk. All of Jacobs's models wore knit beanies, a look that was closer to a yarmulke than the inexpensive knit watch cap favored in the Northwest.

Jacobs had taken over design duties at Perry Ellis International after Ellis's death, but the Grunge collection would prove to be his undoing at the prestigious fashion company; he was fired when his designs failed to sell. "Though [Jacobs] had delivered a much-discussed and much-photographed Grunge-inspired collection for spring, the board of Perry Ellis International did not foresee making money on his women's wear," *The New York Times* reported.

Fans of Grunge music passed on the designs because they thought them overpriced. "Designers co-opted Kurt Cobain's protest and commodified it," wrote Nika Mavrody for *The Fashion Spot,* "marketing a high-fashion version of the Seattle music scene's anti-fashion aesthetic to young people, at exorbitant prices." Another astute observation for their failure came from Walter Thomas, creative director at J. Crew: "By the time you see [a trend] in Kmart, it can be three years [after that trend first hit the catwalk]. The difference with Grunge is that it was *already* for sale at Kmart, not to mention the Salvation Army." The Grunge look had started in Kmart, or thrift stores, but it didn't become trendy until it was worn by a rock icon.

In time, fashion writers began to shift their opinion on Jacobs's designs. Eventually, some fashion blogs hailed his Grunge collection as "ahead of its time" and "genius." Furthermore, some of the creations of other designers during that 1993 season that incorporated Grunge elements, like Anna Sui's, did sell, perhaps because they were influenced by the Grunge look, albeit at higher quality and prices, but weren't a direct copy. When a garment had just a touch of Grunge, like a tattered fringe, it found more acceptance than an entire outfit.

Grunge style, surprisingly, has stuck around. One fashion website recently called Kurt "an avid texture mixer" for contrasting sweaters with ripped jeans. What Marc Jacobs had described as his certain "fucked up"-ness became a style flourish that was hugely influential. The "vintage" look came to every department of the clothing store. As the *Guest of a Guest* fashion website recently opined, "Kurt Cobain took the art of worn-in denim to new extremes . . . Because of this, distressed denim is still on the shelves and racks of stores today." Imagine Urban Outfitters or American Apparel without Grunge-influenced styles.

Furthermore, the word "Grunge" has had a lifetime in fashion, and a cachet it has not enjoyed in popular music. In music, Grunge represents a certain time and place. In fashion, it means a style that is current and still hip. If you searched "Grunge" on Nordstrom's website in late 2013, 141 clothing choices appeared, everything from jackets to sneakers. Even on eBay, a pull-down menu lists "Grunge" as a separate category of clothing. "Grunge" is not listed as a category within music on eBay.

Grunge's biggest fashion impact seems to have been in footwear. In 2013, Amazon listed fifty-three different "Grunge" shoes on their fashion site. Army boots and Doc Martens are ubiquitous. Both Tom's Shoes and Nike issued designs with Sub Pop's logo on them in 2013. Sub Pop Nikes would have been unheard of in 1988, but as the lines between music and fashion blur, Grunge continues as an influence. "Fashion houses used to be run by 'uncool' people, who were very serious about things and didn't understand the role of culture," observed Andrea Linnet. "Now it's a given that what a band wears is going to affect fashion."

High fashion has also continued to market clothes with Grunge influences, at sometimes exorbitant prices. Fashion writers described recent collections by Phillip Lim, Dries Van Noten, Oliver Wang, Peter Som, and even Calvin Klein all as "Grunge." Kurt's name often appears in the press on these new lines of clothes. One five-hundred-word 2003 piece on that season's fashion standouts in *The New York Times* mentioned Kurt five times. Headlined SMELLS LIKE GRUNGE AGAIN, Ruth La Ferla's article opined, "Grunge: that much maligned Seattle-born style, popularized by rock legends like Nirvana, has reared its head once more in the shape of lumberjack shirts, jaunty kilts, beat-up sweat shirts, bleached-out jeans, and all many of leggings in worker-bee stripes . . . Stores like Hot Topic, H&M, and American Eagle chase after teenagers' dollars with work shirts and jeans, meant to be piled on chaotically in the manner of Kurt Cobain."

"Smells Like Grunge Again" also highlighted Jean Touitou's A.P.C. collection, which was titled "Smells Like Seattle." Touitou explained that his designs were in response to "all that cheap glamour" in the rest of fashion. Andrew Bolton, curator of the Costume Institute at the New York Metropolitan Museum of Art, commented, "Grunge returns whenever fashion is reacting against a more preppy or establishment look. It's very much an anti-fashion statement, one that breaks down the notions of what goes with what . . . Today [Grunge] style is romanticized. It's more about nostalgia than politics."

A simple Internet search would reveal numerous fashion blogs that track Grunge styles, including *Fashion. Grunge. Style.* That site's editor, Lauren Brown, said that in the last five years the Grunge look has "grasped the fashion media world like wildfire." Spurred by the financial crisis, shopping at thrift stores for vintage items has never been hipper or more accepted in mainstream fashion. Brown says this round of interest in Grunge "has no clear and defined music style that is attached to the resurgence of the subculture." In a strange about-face, Grunge fashion is now influenced by fashion trendsetters, and not necessarily by musical ones.

Even a model or two has been known to cite Kurt as an influence. The model Agyness Deyn was such a fan of Kurt that when she began designing dresses, one of her first creations was based on a dress Kurt wore onstage. Model Alexa Chung told *The New York Times* that Kurt was one of her "beauty icons." Stylists, she complained, try to make her "hair shiny, and I don't want it. I want to look like Kurt Cobain."

Kurt's influence has increased as younger designers, who grew up worshipping his music, move into power positions and dictate fashion trends. Lauren Brown told me some young designers "even cite certain outfits from live performances and press shoots as inspiration for their collections." The T-shirt company Wornfree makes vintage reproductions of the *Sounds* shirt that Kurt wore in many photo sessions. The forty-five-dollar T-shirt comes with a picture showing Kurt wearing the same design.

Grunge's biggest year on the runway may have been in

2012–2013, when several highly regarded lines also jumped on the bandwagon. Givenchy's Fall 2013 collection included its "Grunge" "Slim Fit Contrast Geometric Front and Yoke Plaid Shirt." It was, for $545, essentially a fancy flannel shirt. Design firm Opening Ceremony launched several high-end shoes in 2013 with Grunge in their title, including the $300 "Grunge Sneaker." Hedi Slimane's Fall 2012 collection for Saint Laurent (formerly Yves Saint Laurent) was described as "Grunge" by more fashion writers than any line since Marc Jacobs's 1993 collection.

One of Slimane's designs was a $6,000 houndstooth trench coat. Another outfit was clearly modeled after one of Courtney Love's baby doll dresses that Kurt wore over his own clothes at a concert. Slimane consciously chose Courtney, Sonic Youth's Kim Gordon, and Marilyn Manson to wear his designs in the initial wave of print ads.

"Hedi nailed it," Courtney Love told me in 2013. "He totally knows Grunge, and he's mixed it into fashion. He's the one guy who got it right. It might be a six-thousand-dollar trench coat, but it is so beautifully made, with such fine fabric, you notice the quality." Still, Love did find it some-what absurd that fashion had gone full circle, and that what she and others bought at thrift stores was now reinterpreted for runways at high prices. She told *New York* magazine, "I just find it hilarious that in three months' time, or however long it takes, women are gonna pay six thousand dollars for a fucking trench coat that cost us $4.99 back in the day. [But Hedi Slimane] got that look absolutely right."

Even Marc Jacobs recovered from his initial 1993 Grunge collection bomb. He took some of the same ideas explored in his Grunge line and opened his own storefront design studio. In that context—high-end, limited production, exclusive contact with a designer, almost as if you were buying fashion from an art gallery—Jacobs did very well. He joined Louis Vuitton in 1997, and in 2010 *Time* magazine named him one of the hundred most influential people in the world. In 2013, he became Diet Coke's creative director.

If Marc Jacobs's $300 flannel shirt failed to ignite sales in 1993, that isn't to say that Grunge didn't fuel apparel sales when Kurt was alive. Low-priced flannel shirts saw a boom, moving from the confines of army-navy surplus and outdoor hunting emporiums into trendy youth-oriented boutiques in the mall. Flannel shirts had always been available at Walmart and Kmart, but they now were on those store's endcaps. Flannel also began to show up at trendy retailers like the Gap and J. Crew.

Many styles of jeans began to exhibit the "distressed look" as a premium finish, not a sign of age or wear. People paid extra to get jeans that looked like what Kurt had bought in a thrift store.

Not long after the Grunge look, another bizarre fashion trend that earned the title "heroin chic" came into fashion advertising. Epitomized by model Kate Moss and an ad campaign launched by Calvin Klein in 1997, a series of advertisements made use of underweight models who appeared drug-addicted, with sunken cheeks and pale skin. In other words, the female Kurt Cobain, circa 1992. The look was controversial, but that didn't mean it wasn't influential, and it played into the trend of anorexic models.

Kurt had passed away by the time of heroin chic, but his death, and his public struggles with addiction, most certainly played a role in the outcry that followed, if not in the trend of heroin chic itself. Having seen a superstar of his magnitude struggle with drugs, the response to Klein's heroin-chic ads was outrage. Thirteen of fashion's biggest names formed Designers Against Addiction and condemned models being portrayed as drug addicts. President Bill Clinton chimed in: "The glorification of heroin is not creative . . . And this is not about art; it's about life and death." Klein discontinued the ad campaign, though the problem of underweight models continues. Designer Karl Lagerfeld said in 2009 that people protesting anorexic models had weight problems themselves. "These are fat mummies sitting with their bags of crisps in front of the television, saying that thin models are ugly," he said.

Kurt Cobain would have taken a different view from Lagerfeld's, or Calvin Klein's. His own thinness made him appear sexy in a society where skinniness was valued, but it was one of the greatest sources of shame for him. Because of his natural thinness, Kurt was accused of being a junkie for years before he became one. Kurt had Calvin Klein's heroin-chic look down, and it was part of what made him a fashion icon, but there was almost nothing about his life he felt more embarrassed about.

How many clothes Kurt helped sell in the nineties can't be measured, but it is easy to trace Kurt's impact on the success of Converse shoes. The company had been in and out of bankruptcy, but in the nineties its sales soared. In 2003, Nike bought Converse for $305 million.

Kurt was not the only rock star associated with Converse, but he nearly lived in the brand. Look at any picture of Kurt, and he is almost certainly wearing Converse. Not since basketball player Chuck Taylor had supplied his name to All Stars in the 1920s had the brand had such an effective celebrity spokesperson, and in Kurt's case one who worked for free.

That brand connection was forever linked in the most awful way, but one that nonetheless proved enduring: Kurt died wearing Converse One Stars. A *Seattle Times* photographer captured a shot of Kurt lying dead in his greenhouse, and it was published on the front page of the *Times* and went out on wire services around the world (other, more grisly shots have since surfaced on the Internet). In the photograph, Kurt's lifeless corpse rests on the floor, still wearing the Converse One Stars. He had tied the laces well, itself a troubling concept when one tries to imagine a suicidal person in their last moments on earth. It was not the kind of association any company would ever seek, but the connection between Converse and Kurt was forever cemented with that death-scene image.

Most kids didn't buy Converse just because Kurt wore them on *Saturday Night Live*, or in the "Smells Like Teen Spirit" video, or died in them, but all of those moments must have played a role in his association with the brand.

I was given an opportunity to examine all of Kurt's possessions after his death—the things he owned, or at least all that remained of them. He had jeans, T-shirts, a few overcoats, and a few pairs of Converse. Kurt had written ENDORSEMENT on the toe of one pair. It was typical Kurt Cobain self-referential sarcastic humor, but in writing that one word, Kurt was saying he knew his footwear choice would matter to millions. And it did.

In going through thousands of photos of Kurt, I never came across a single picture that showed him wearing this particular pair of shoes, but his graffiti was small enough that it would have been hidden from almost any angle except directly above. These were relatively new Converses, by Kurt's standards, so they were probably purchased in the last few months of his life. They had maybe three months' worth of wear, and the ENDORSEMENT mark had started to come off a bit. Kurt did not treat these sneakers like the museum piece they one day will most likely be (they are currently kept in a secure climate-controlled vault). As with every piece of clothes or footwear he owned, he beat the crap out of them.

Kurt's writing on the end of his shoe would play a small role in yet another controversy involving him. In 2006, the music publishing and marketing firm Primary Wave acquired 25 percent of the Kurt Cobain music catalog from Courtney Love. Love sold this share for several reasons, one being that she needed the money to pay off her debts—but also, at least she argued to me, because she felt that as the years went by, and Nirvana's music was rarely used in movies or television shows, it became less vital, important, and maybe even less valuable. That same year, Love and the remaining members of Nirvana licensed "All Apologies" to the HBO television show *Six Feet Under.* "Something in the Way" also appeared in the movie *Jarhead.* Both uses were written about in the press and drew largely positive notices, though some fans felt they were exploitation.

Primary Wave manages and markets the music-publishing interests of many superstars and estates, including Bo Diddley, Chicago, Def Leppard, Hall and Oates, Daniel Johnston,

Gregg Allman, John Lennon, Steve Earle, and Steven Tyler. Still, buying the Cobain music-publishing rights was Primary Wave's biggest and most public acquisition. The purchase price was large enough that Kurt rose to the number one spot on *Forbes*'s list of lucrative dead celebrities, above Elvis Presley and John Lennon.

Love's then manager Peter Asher told *Forbes*, "We believe if we say yes to the right things, we can do both—make money, and do the right thing for the catalog." Asher said the public's attitudes toward licensing had shifted, as bands like U2 and the Rolling Stones regularly sold songs to commercials. "Now it's, 'Oh cool, they're using my favorite band,'" Asher said. Primary Wave CEO Lawrence Mestel, former head of Virgin Records, told *Forbes* he would only license Kurt's image to the appropriate sources. "You will never see Kurt Cobain's music in a fast-food hamburger advertisement," Mestel said. One of the first, and so far one of the only, places Primary Wave has licensed Kurt's name has been the most obvious: Converse sneakers.

In early 2008, Converse announced it was issuing authorized "Kurt Cobain edition" shoes. The line was a limited run in the Converse Century campaign. There were two styles in the Kurt Cobain line: one featured "vintage-ized" versions of the Chuck Taylor All Star, One Star, and Jack Purcell models, while the other was a line of All Stars with Kurt's writings and sketches on them. The insoles featured the phrase "punk rock means freedom" in Kurt's handwriting. The shoes were priced from $50 to $65 a pair. Converse also announced they were making shoes with designs by the Grateful Dead and the Doors.

Many Nirvana fans were outraged, feeling that any item with Kurt's name attached, even when the brand was Converse, was exploitive. Primary Wave's Devin Lasker defended the product to the press: "Kurt wore these shoes." Still, as *Ad Age* blogger Charlie Morgan pointed out at the time, "He died in the things. I mean, that's disturbing."

Lead singer of Seattle band Death Cab for Cutie Ben Gibbard weighed in to *Details*: "When I was a teenager, the idea of Kurt Cobain having his own sneaker—that would've been like sacrilege," Gibbard said. But even Gibbard, who like many musicians in Seattle looked upon Kurt as a role model, understood the scope of this particular endorsement. "If they were making 'Heart-Shaped Box' into 'Eight-Piece Box' for, like, Kentucky Fried Chicken, yeah, that would offend me. But if it takes a Kurt Cobain Converse to remind people to go buy Nirvana records, that's fine with me."

The Kurt Cobain Converse sneakers sold well. Every version of the line, and every model, eventually sold out. The sneakers now sell for a premium on eBay.

It was initially jarring to me to think about a Kurt Cobain–branded product, but if Kurt was going to endorse anything, it would have been Converse. He probably would have given his authorization if they'd sent him a couple of free pairs. In the end I warmed to the idea, particularly thinking of Kurt's ENDORSEMENT written on the end of his shoe. I couldn't bring myself to buy a pair, though.

If there ever was a compelling case for the power of Kurt Cobain's name and how valuable that connection is still considered by marketers, it came with Dr. Martens shoes. If Kurt's name on a product he liked caused controversy for Converse, imagine what happened around an advertisement that evoked his name and image for something he never wore. Thus the 2007 shit storm that sprang up when Dr. Martens decided to use Kurt's name and likeness without permission in an ad.

A German army doctor in World War II had designed Dr. Martens boots and shoes, but by the 1960s they were the go-to boots for the English working class. The boots became the choice for UK youth including the Teddy Boys, skin-heads, and, eventually, punk rockers. They were imported to the US, but in the 1980s only a couple of stores in Seat-tle sold them. One was the retail outlet where Soundgarden's Chris Cornell's then girlfriend and later wife worked. It is no surprise, then, that Cornell wore Dr. Martens, as did Pearl Jam's Eddie Vedder and Layne Staley of Alice in Chains (both of those later bands were managed, or advised, by Cornell's wife). When Grunge took off as a cultural phenomenon after *Nevermind* exploded, and Seattle rockers were photographed wearing Docs, sales of the brand skyrocketed. Soon Doc Mar-tens were being sold in Seattle's Nordstrom.

Kurt Cobain's association with Dr. Martens, however, was distant at best. If a photograph exists of him wearing Docs, I've not seen it. No Dr. Martens were in his personal effects that I had the privilege to see. Prior to 1992 Kurt had no money, and Docs, which still cost $100 a pair in that era, were beyond his pre-*Nevermind* means. When I asked Courtney if Kurt ever wore them, her response was "NEVER." But Dr. Martens nonetheless became a fashion choice so strongly as-sociated with Grunge that they became associated with Kurt. This fact did not escape the advertising agency Saatchi & Saat-chi. In 2007, as part of the Dr. Martens Forever campaign, the agency put together a series of ads in Great Britain that featured illustrations of legendary rock stars—including Kurt, Joe Strummer, Sid Vicious, and Joey Ramone—in heaven, sitting on a cloud, with their Docs on.

The ads immediately drew attention, which was probably exactly what Dr. Martens had hoped for, but the discourse went off track when Nirvana fans complained loudly that Kurt never wore the shoes. Even if he had, the idea of Kurt in an advertisement, particularly one that showed him in heaven with combat boots on, was in horrible taste. Fans of the Clash also complained, but the protests about Kurt were loudest, as if he had the highest sanctity.

Courtney called the ads "outrageous" and demanded they be taken down. Love said Dr. Martens was trying "to commercially gain from such a despicable use" of Kurt's picture for a product he didn't use. The Cobain estate had not approved the ad, nor had anyone associated with Nirvana. They were allowed because UK law doesn't protect the rights of publicity of deceased celebrities in product endorsements. To add insult to injury, the ads appeared on some US websites, where their legal basis was less solid. The advertising agency called that a "mistake."

Given the brouhaha that followed, it was no surprise that

Dr. Martens fired its advertising agency and issued a public apology. "We are really, really, really sorry," Dr. Martens CEO David Suddens said, with rare forthrightness for a corporate head. "We do think that it is offensive. We made a mistake. My message to Courtney Love is: this is something we shouldn't have been doing." A Saatchi & Saatchi spokesperson defended the ads, saying, "We believe the ads are edgy, but not offensive."

The Dr. Martens controversy shows how powerful and important Kurt Cobain's endorsement is still perceived to be within the marketplace, and that Kurt's integrity is still a valuable entity. What Kurt wore mattered, and still matters, to millions of fans, to apparel marketers, and to high-fashion designers. His individual fashion sense—however accidental, however rooted in practicality and necessity—created ripples that are still being felt within the apparel industry. Kurt Cobain may be long gone from this world, but from the catwalk to casual styles sold at Target, his choices in clothing are still having an impact.

FOUR

THE PERFECT SEATTLE MOMENT
Aberdeen & Seattle

Kurt Cobain was born in Aberdeen, Washington, in 1967. Despite his strong association with Seattle, he only lived in that city for eighteen months. He spent twenty years in Aberdeen, though, or in surrounding Grays Harbor County. His work and life were shaped by his time in Aberdeen, and he, in turn, transformed Aberdeen.

The most powerful music always comes with a sense of place that informs both the musician creating the song and the listener hearing it. A song's setting is an entry into our imagination and a way to turn the singer's world into our own. Sometimes place is specifically evoked in a song's lyrics, as in Otis Redding's "Sittin' on the Dock of the Bay," or it may be used as metaphor, as in Bob Dylan's "Stuck Inside of Mobile with the Memphis Blues Again." And sometimes a song is set in an emotional place, an internal world with no physical address.

Kurt Cobain wrote roughly one hundred songs, and nearly half of those were either written in Aberdeen or informed by imagery from the city. No song is as closely connected with both Aberdeen's physical place and Kurt's emotional connection to it as "Something in the Way," from *Nevermind*. The enduring power of this song with listeners—and the lure of the actual physical place to fans—illustrates how Kurt's work transformed one tiny, real part of the world.

"Something in the Way" uses only nine lines of unique lyrics and is remarkably simple in structure. The chorus repeats the title's four words, with Kurt stretching out every syllable with a deliberateness of pronunciation that is in complete contrast to how he sings "Smells Like Teen Spirit." The song's narrator is underneath a bridge, where his tarp has "sprung a leak," and he is living off "drippings from the ceiling." A listener travels to the emotional center of a man who feels his presence in the world is an impediment rather than a blessing.

It succeeds because the minor chords perfectly suit lyrics about the universal feeling of disconnection. This was a common theme for Kurt, and a central one in his catalog of songs.

The lyrics of "Something in the Way" don't actually mention Aberdeen, but Kurt said in several interviews he had written the song about when he was homeless and living "under a bridge." He didn't actually "live" there, as the bridge in Aberdeen he was referring to crosses a tidal river, which means the water ebbs twice a day, and Kurt was too sensitive a sort to live outside in any case. Still, Kurt's explanation became a central one to his mythology, as did the bridge itself. The Young Street Bridge sits just two blocks away from Kurt's childhood home, a fact that itself says much about how disconnected he felt from his family. The bridge is only a hundred meters long and looks no different on its surface from the road on either side. The underside is visually striking only because concrete pillars rise from the water to stand next to rotted supports from an old pier. The effect is of many broken vertical shapes, askew in different angles.

The Young Street Bridge spans the Wishkah River, a small tidal offshoot of the larger Chehalis. The Wishkah River's water is muddy, opaque, and always brown from tidal runoff, and the spot also inspired the title to the 1996 Nirvana live album *From the Muddy Banks of the Wishkah*. There are just thirty square yards of riverbank under the Young Street Bridge, enough for a dozen people to sit, but when the water rises, that space is greatly reduced.

Kurt spent some time here as a teenager, where it served as a sanctuary from the world of adults and a place of reflection. Nirvana fans have inflated the legend of the bridge because of Kurt's stories about it, and because of the many incorrect rumors that the bridge was where he first did heroin. Kurt experimented with drugs in Aberdeen, but probably the most he ever did under the bridge was smoke pot or get drunk.

The underside of the bridge already had graffiti during Kurt's time, some painted by him, but it has become a shrine of sorts now: every square inch of available space is filled with messages from fans to, or about, Kurt, many in foreign languages. It has become a way station along the Nirvana fan pilgrimage and one of the most popular tourist attractions in Aberdeen. Fans come seeking a part of Kurt, and the tiny underside of the bridge is the most significant landmark they can locate in his hometown.

Kurt is long gone from Aberdeen, and from this world.

Still, the Young Street Bridge remains connected to him, transformed by a song.

Aberdeen, Washington, could not be a more unlikely place for a rock star to grow up. It was settled by trappers but became a center for timber because the natural harbor offered easy access to the nearby Pacific Ocean. That fueled initial development, but its remote location—two hours from Seattle—stymied large-scale growth. Most early logging operations were clear-cuts, which felled large swaths of virgin timber and ultimately damaged the habitat for endangered species like the spotted owl. The most obvious effects of the practice of clear-cutting are the huge swaths of stumps that cover hillsides near Aberdeen, unexpected ugliness in a region of majestic natural beauty.

Kurt grew up in an era when the timber industry was already on the decline, and unemployment was nearly twice as high in Aberdeen as in other parts of Washington State. Overfishing and overlogging had depleted remaining resources, and numerous attempts by various entities to develop more diverse employment bases had been mostly unsuccessful. One of the only recent growth industries has been a prison that opened in 2000 and has become among Aberdeen's largest employers.

When Kurt was born on February 20, 1967, his father worked at a service station. They lived at 2830½ Aberdeen Avenue in nearby Hoquiam, though Kurt was born at the hospital in Aberdeen. The Cobains eventually moved to a house in the northeast part of Aberdeen, near the Young Street Bridge, in a neighborhood nicknamed Felony Flats because many local troublemakers lived there. Kurt himself was arrested twice during his time in Aberdeen, for graffiti and possessing alcohol as a minor.

That "half" address of 2830½ Aberdeen Avenue, where Kurt lived as a baby, would prove to be a trend. It was one of five homes in which Kurt would reside over the span of his life with "half" addresses: they were all shacks or cabins or parts of apartments or converted garages that had been carved out of other proper houses. In that manner, nearly every house Kurt ever lived in, with just a few exceptions, had a something-in-the-way feel, as if they were tacked on to other residences, never true homes—and those who lived there were just on the edge of homelessness.

Aberdeen was itself a city Kurt thought was disconnected from the rest of the world by culture and economics, but sometimes it was literally isolated. The main road into Aberdeen abuts a cliff, and occasionally, after heavy rains, a rock or mud slide blocks the road. On those days, Aberdeen isn't just metaphorically isolated from the rest of the world—it is physically cut off, too.

Johnny Marr, the guitar player of the Smiths and later Modest Mouse, told me he had a theory that the influential music cities of Northern England and Washington State had commonalities. "They share working-class economics," he told me, "and the kind of people who live in a rainy city." To Marr, both Manchester and Seattle create or attract a certain breed of musician, one with an edge. "It's more than just the gray sky and the rain," he observed. "It's more about the attitude. It's an indoor culture in both those places." Both Seattle and Manchester are known for guitar-based rock with dense layers of vocals, distortion effects, and drum beats that often shift tempo rather than lay down a consistent rhythm.

And if Marr's observation on indoor culture is true for Seattle and Manchester, it is even truer for Aberdeen, which gets eighty-four inches of rain a year, twice that of Seattle or Manchester. Aberdeen's extreme weather has always gone hand in hand with a preference for harder music—garage rock and heavy metal. "By the early sixties, Grays Harbor was a hotbed of garage rock," John Hughes, the former publisher of the Aberdeen *Daily World* newspaper, told me. Hughes also observed links between the region and Northern England: "Grays Harbor has a gritty, Liverpool-like appetite for loud, live music."

The first Aberdeen band to be signed to a major label wasn't Nirvana but the thrash-metal band Metal Church. Their self-titled debut in 1984 sold seventy thousand copies and was picked up by Elektra Records. Kurt Cobain grew up a fan of that band—he liked thrash, and death metal, too. He also most likely took his frequent alternative spelling of his own name, Kurdt, from Metal Church's lead singer, Kurdt Vanderhoof.

A bigger local influence on Kurt, though, were the Melvins, who sold very few records in the eighties but provided him the template for punk rock itself. When Kurt first saw the Melvins perform in a grocery-store parking lot in Montesano, Washington (the band took its name from the manager of that grocery store), just a few miles east of Aberdeen, he wrote in his journal, "This was what I was looking for." He wrote it twice, and underlined it.

The Melvins played around Aberdeen for a few years but made very little money. (Kurt would help get them a major-label record deal with Atlantic in 1993, and even coproduced their *Houdini* album; one of his first publicly displayed artworks was a portrait of the members of the band Kiss painted on the side of the Melvins' band van, the Mel-Van.) In 1988 the Melvins left Aberdeen, as Kurt had done just months before: he moved sixty miles west to Olympia in 1987, and it was there where he wrote most of the songs that would end up on *Nevermind*. Though he'd return to his hometown for the occasional gig or to visit friends and family, Kurt wouldn't live in Aberdeen again.

When Nirvana rose to international attention in 1991, so did Aberdeen. The city was often featured when the media first began to profile the band. Many Aberdeen residents were not comfortable with the association, particularly in light of the fact that Kurt repeatedly talked about Aberdeen as if it was filled with hicks. In one band biography release he wrote for Nirvana in 1988, Kurt described Aberdeen as full of "highly-bigoted redneck snoose-chewing deer-shooting faggot-killing logger-types who ain't too partial to 'weirdo new wavers.'"

Needless to say, Kurt did not win fans at the Aberdeen Chamber of Commerce with this depiction of his hometown.

Things soured further in 1992 when Kurt's drug addiction became news. Though drinking and taverns were central to Aberdeen life, newspaper stories about heroin embarrassed the town's leaders because their association with Kurt was still so strong. Of course, Kurt's suicide in 1994 brought the kind of infamy few towns would seek. "Some joked that it was a revolting development for Aberdeen to be famous for Nirvana," says John Hughes. Aberdeen had already had run-ins with media stereotypes in previous decades. The town's downtown core was once so populated with brothels that in 1952 *Look* magazine cited it as "one of the hotspots in America's battle against sin." Residents seemed quicker to embrace that ribald past (a local tavern even sold T-shirts that read ABERDEEN WHOREHOUSE RESTORATION SOCIETY) than their connection with Kurt. There were several attempts immediately after Kurt's death to have something officially named after Kurt in Aberdeen, but all failed outright. One local sculptor created a statute of Kurt, but the city wouldn't allow it on a public street. Eventually, the statue was put on display inside a muffler-repair shop.

Aberdeen doesn't have a bookstore that holds literary

events, so when I did a reading for *Heavier Than Heaven* there in 2001, it was held at the library. That was appropriate in a way, as Kurt passed many days of his youth reading books in that building. There was one element, however, that I wasn't expecting: protestors. One held a sign that said, DON'T GLORIFY DRUGGIES. But this being Aberdeen, with a small-town friendliness even in matters of heated debate, that particular protestor ended up coming to the reading and buying my book anyway. My impression of Aberdeen residents over the years has been a little different from Kurt's experience. I've run into "snoose-chewing" rednecks, but I've also met many educated, well-read intellectuals. Many are even proud of their famous musicians.

But not all. In 2004, for the ten-year anniversary of Kurt's death, the mayor of nearby Hoquiam put forward a proclamation honoring Kurt. The proclamation was essentially a piece of paper stating that Kurt lived in the town as a baby, and issuing it officially would have cost the city nothing. It failed to pass when some suggested it would signal a public endorsement of drug use. "What kind of message is this sending to my kids?" Hoquiam city council member Tom Plumb asked.

In the past decade, that perception of Kurt has begun to shift in Aberdeen, and surrounding Grays Harbor County.

"Even the naysayers have warmed up to the idea that Nirvana was a transformative band, and a real source of pride," John Hughes observed. Some of that shift came as motel and restaurant owners noticed a steady stream of visiting Nirvana fans. Some of the change, I suspect, reflects a wider national trend: as the sensationalistic aspects of Kurt's life and death fade further into the past, his work becomes the larger part of his current history. Kurt's musical legacy, easier to embrace for politicians than his personal demons, also brings much needed tourist dollars to the struggling city.

In 2004, three Aberdeen High School students wrote a story in the daily newspaper asking why their city had never done anything to officially honor Kurt Cobain. That same year, one of the newspaper's writers and a city council member formed the nonprofit Kurt Cobain Memorial Committee. Their first goal was to place a sign at the city limits saying that Aberdeen was the birthplace of Kurt, but that was deemed too controversial. Eventually the committee raised private money to construct a small addition to the existing "Welcome to Aberdeen" sign that would read: "Come As You Are." The organizers gambled that by mentioning Kurt's iconic song, and not his name, they might have a greater chance of getting official approval. "We were looking to honor a guy who had said some rather mean things about his hometown and the people who lived there," Jeff Burlingame, an Aberdeen author and co-organizer of the effort, told me. "Many were not fond of that, nor were they fond of his lifestyle or his means of death." But the city council approved the effort, and it was installed at the city limits. It has since become an iconic part of Aberdeen's identity.

Over the years there have been other attempts to construct a more overt memorial in Aberdeen, or to possibly name a street or a park after Kurt. A proposal to rename the Young Street Bridge the Kurt Cobain Bridge was voted down ten to one by the city council. "Is this the legacy we want to leave to our children?" local pastor Don Eden said at the time.

In 2008, a senior citizen who lived next to the Young Street Bridge became frustrated at attitudes like Eden's and took matters into his own hands. Tori Kovach cleared out a half acre of blackberry bushes from city property near the path to the underside of the bridge and began the process of creating a "park" there with his bare hands. Other locals started to help, and businesses donated materials. This do-it-yourself attitude, which Kurt had as well, is one of the things I admire about the citizens of Aberdeen. A sign was constructed in etched metal that featured the lyrics of "Something in the Way" on it. Kovach told *The Daily World* he was more of a fan of Elvis Presley than Kurt Cobain, but Aberdeen was overdue to recognize Kurt. "Aspects of his life resonate with me because I was from a broken home," Kovach said. The citizen-created park stirred some to complain, but eventually the city voted to take it over. The spot is now officially the Kurt Cobain Riverfront Park.

In 2013 a proposal was put forth to the Aberdeen city council to demolish the "Come As You Are" sign. After some consideration, the council voted unanimously to keep it as is. And when the Kurt Cobain Memorial Committee has organized benefit concerts, they've been well attended and supported by donations from some of the nearby governments, including even Hoquiam's. "Today, anyone from Aberdeen who speaks of Kurt in a negative light on social media will find himself shouted down tenfold," Jeff Burlingame says. "Time, as it does with most things, has softened the spite. The line graph of Kurt's popularity in Aberdeen, if there were such a thing, would still be heading north." John Hughes agrees: "With every passing year, Aberdeen has come to grips with his genius."

A sign at Aberdeen's Kurt Cobain Riverfront Park also notes that it is one of the many spots Kurt's ashes were scattered after his cremation. It reads, in part: KURT IMMORTALIZED THIS RIVER. IN TURN, THE RIVER NOW IMMORTALIZES HIM.

Seattle's relationship with Kurt was, and remains, markedly different from Aberdeen's. "Seattle band Nirvana" was the description in nearly every story or news report on the band after they became famous. That Nirvana were from Aberdeen had been detailed in local publications like my magazine *The Rocket,* but as Nirvana became an international sensation, their hometown was often left out of the history. Sometimes when Aberdeen was mentioned in that 1991 wave of press, it was incorrectly described as "just outside" Seattle, when the cities were worlds away culturally and two hours by distance. I've even seen it written, likely by journalists who never visited the Northwest, that Aberdeen was a "suburb" of Seattle, something that would cause a howl of laughter to any resident from either of those cities. But to most of the world outside the Northwest, "Seattle" and "Nirvana" were synonymous.

At the start of 1991, though, only one member of Nirvana lived in Seattle, and that was Dave Grohl. Grohl had moved there a month before the release of *Nevermind* after growing tired of sleeping on the sofa in Kurt's tiny Olympia apartment. Krist Novoselic lived in Tacoma that year and didn't buy a Seattle home until *Nevermind*'s royalties started arriving in 1992. "We couldn't afford to live in Seattle," Novoselic told me. Kurt certainly couldn't afford Seattle rents: he had a hard time scraping up $200 to pay for his apartment in Olympia. When he returned home after recording *Nevermind* in California, he'd been evicted for back-due rent. He'd just recorded an album that would go on to sell thirty-five million copies, but on the day he arrived home, all his possessions were in boxes on the curb. He slept in his car for the next week until he started rooming with friends, and eventually in hotel rooms paid for by his record label as Nirvana began to tour.

For much of 1991 and 1992, Kurt continued to stay in hotels and crash with friends as Nirvana toured more regularly. His next semipermanent address was in Los Angeles, where he and Courtney Love rented an apartment awaiting the birth of Frances Bean Cobain in August 1992. They had intended to stay in Los Angeles only temporarily, but when California Child Protective Services became involved in their lives due to rumors of their drug use that had appeared in *Vanity Fair,* they couldn't move out of the state. They stayed in a few different temporary apartments, but the one they resided in the longest was in the Fairfax neighborhood. Their apartment had a large picture window, but the drapes were never opened. In one of the sunniest places in the United States, Kurt brought Aberdeen with him.

Kurt and Courtney, with baby in tow, didn't move to Seattle until late 1992, living initially in fancy hotels. They repeatedly ran into trouble with hotel management—smoking violations, damages, drug activity, unpaid bills—and were essentially kicked out of every four-star hotel in Seattle. They rented a house in northeast Seattle for the next year, which was to be their most permanent Seattle domicile. It wasn't until January 1994 that they bought their mansion in the Denny-Blaine neighborhood of Seattle. It was the first home Kurt ever owned, and it would be the last: he would die in the greenhouse-type room above the garage just three months after purchasing the house.

Seattle was in many ways ideally suited to Kurt's personality and his moment of fame. The Seattle music scene was created organically—no one imagined it would become as big as it did, and thus egos were left at the door. After Nirvana struck, I'd often find myself escorting visiting New York–based journalists who wanted to see the sights of where this red-hot music "scene" had developed. But there was little to see, as the scene had come together in mostly basements and garages. Almost every other vital music scene in the nation—from Austin to Los Angeles's Sunset Strip—had developed because of a strong local club circuit. Seattle bands broke through for the opposite reason: there *wasn't* a decent club scene. Since bands couldn't make money playing live, they retreated to basements to rehearse and imagined that recording a single or an album would be their ticket to stardom. It was the very fact that there was no chance of success and riches from playing live that forced these groups to aim higher, to go straight to making a record. And it worked.

When bands could scrape up enough luck to land a gig at one of the handful of Seattle clubs that booked original bands, audiences would inevitably number in the dozens, and everyone in the crowd knew each other. A tribe mentality existed that was insular but also nurturing. Most audience members at venues like the Vogue or the Central Tavern were members of other bands. "We played at the time not thinking we'd be successful or famous," Soundgarden's guitarist Kim Thayil once told me, "but simply because we wanted to impress our friends. It was a scene built on friendships, and that's one reason bands were so supportive of each other and not competitive." Consequently, there was no place in town for big egos and judgment, and status within the Seattle music scene, at least through the mid-nineties, was afforded only for talent, not for fame or money.

This was perfectly suited to Kurt Cobain's attitude. Although he desperately wanted to succeed, he didn't want to be too obvious about it. That was the source of Kurt's beef with Pearl Jam: he felt that band had sinned by overtly wanting success. In the press, Kurt delivered what would be the sternest rebuke for a Seattle band: he called Pearl Jam "careerists." (He described them in *Rolling Stone* as a "corporate, alternative and cock-rock fusion" band.) It was hypocrisy, of course, as Kurt could have easily stuck with independent record labels, but in truth he wanted to sell albums as much as anyone. Kurt, and Nirvana, left Sub Pop and signed with the "corporate" major label Geffen because they wanted the money that deal brought. But in Seattle, "desire" was a dirty word, and Kurt downplayed his.

In turn, even when Nirvana were incredibly famous, Seattleites treated Kurt as if he were a member of any other band, superstar or not. I was in Seattle clubs a dozen times when Kurt, or one of the other members of Nirvana, was present. Yes, muffled whispers would pass through the crowd that royalty was in the house, but no one would dare do something as lame as ask Kurt for an autograph, or a photograph, or harass him in any way. Even when Kurt was a huge superstar, he was given a kind of anonymity in Seattle that he could not have found anywhere else. And Kurt made himself easy to spot: though many in Seattle music dressed in essentially the same uniform—jeans, T-shirts, sneakers—in the last year of his life, Kurt frequently wore an Elmer Fudd–style hunting cap with flaps. The hat stood out on the streets of Seattle, and so did the most famous rock star in the world who was wearing it. But still, nobody bothered him.

If there is one story that most illustrates the essence of Seattle, it came when Courtney decided the couple needed a new car. She didn't drive, but Kurt had two vintage cars, an old Valiant and a Volvo. So they went out together and bought a brand-new black Lexus. They were worth millions then and could have afforded a fleet of luxury cars. But Kurt drove the Lexus for less than a day before he became uncomfortable with the showiness of it.

He returned the Lexus to the dealership, claiming he didn't like the color, and got his money back. Kurt then took a cab back to his million-dollar mansion. His beater cars were still parked in the driveway.

If Seattle was the ideal city for Kurt Cobain to be a star, it was also true that Kurt Cobain was the ideal rock star for Seattle. Nirvana's rise, and the attention that Grunge music received internationally, was perfectly timed for Seattle's big star turn. The explosion of Seattle music came at exactly the moment Microsoft, Starbucks, and Amazon were all bringing attention to the city. In prior decades, Seattle had primarily been known in business circles as the home of Boeing, and in music culture as the hometown of Jimi Hendrix. The only local band that had found platinum record success before 1991 was Heart. And even though Seattle served as headquarters for several Fortune 500 companies, prior to the nineties its unofficial symbol was the Space Needle, a UFO-shaped icon constructed for the 1962 World's Fair.

Nirvana was only one band, and one aspect, of Seattle's coming-out party in 1991, but *Nevermind* may have earned the town more national press than anything other than Microsoft that year. Record companies began to scour the Seattle music scene looking for talent, and in many cases they found it. "No one can get a seat on a plane to Seattle or Portland now," said Ed Rosenblatt of Geffen Records at the time. "Every flight is booked by A&R people out to find the next Nirvana." In the year following *Nevermind,* Pearl Jam, Soundgarden, and

Alice in Chains all earned platinum records of their own. And the good news for Seattle was that every one of those bands actually resided in the city, and unlike Nirvana those bands deserved the connection.

The particular artistic sensibility of Kurt Cobain also struck a chord with Seattle residents and tastemakers. The city has always appreciated the underdog, the left-of-center artist, the outlier. "There's something deeper here, less about money, more about art," Knute Berger, a columnist for *Seattle* magazine, told me. Berger cites influential Northwest painters Mark Tobey and Morris Graves, poets Theodore Roethke and William Stafford, and other artistic types who were connected to the Northwest's working-class roots but who were also doing world-class work. Grunge's ascent gave Seattle a sense that it had a chance to be famous for something other than rain, software, or coffee. "Muddy, mucky, dark indigenous art could still happen here, burst forth, and capture the world's attention," Berger said. "Culture and validation: the perfect Seattle moment."

If there was a moment in time when that validation was most obvious, at least when it came to commercial success, it was the summer of 1994, the year Kurt died. In that year alone, four different Seattle bands—Nirvana, Alice in Chains,

Pearl Jam, and Soundgarden—topped the *Billboard* sales charts. There has not been a year since when a quartet of bands from one region of the world all scored No. 1 albums. "At that moment," Soundgarden's Kim Thayil told me, "it felt like the Seattle Mariners had just won the World Series in baseball. It started to seem like something was happening, not just to me, but to Seattle."

It was an indelible time, one that has stayed with Seattle ever since. Music became a part of Seattle's identity—apparently a permanent part, if the last two decades were a sign of things to come. Musicians from around the country, by the van-load, moved to Seattle. Some of them became famous, some didn't, but an infrastructure of record labels, music attorneys, recording studios, managers, booking agents, and live music venues developed, none of which had been in place in the eighties. The club scene—once so lame that Sub Pop bands were driven to rehearse in basements rather than play live—burst forth and became world-class. Seattle's superstar bands would only play in those clubs for "surprise," announced-at-the-last-minute shows, but the clubs were packed every night of the week with all the B-level bands who were hoping for greatness, along with their fans.

At *The Rocket* we published a directory of working Northwest bands once a year. In the late eighties there were three hundred bands on that list, identifying themselves as "working" bands and not just pickup groups; by the early nineties that number had mushroomed to a thousand. Within those listings were a dozen bands whose members would be next in the long line of famous Northwest groups: Built to Spill, the Presidents of the United States, Seven Year Bitch, Elliott Smith, Supersuckers, Harvey Danger, Candlebox, Sleater-Kinney, Modest Mouse, Neko Case, MxPx, the Shins, Band of Horses, Walking Papers. From that early-nineties scene even came some of the musicians who would later play in the band with the biggest breakthrough of 2013, Macklemore, whose megahit "Thrift Shop" could be the first musical ode to Grunge fashion. Macklemore himself was too young to have been listed in *The Rocket*'s nineties-era directory of bands, but the man who sings the chorus of "Thrift Shop," Michael "Wanz" Wansley, was there.

It wasn't Kurt Cobain who made these bands that followed Nirvana successful—it was their talent—but the ground he broke, and the attention Nirvana brought to Seattle, helped get some of this music heard. Nirvana was a big enough tanker in the water of the music industry that many other bands saw their boats rise with them.

For me, the crystalizing moment that proved that my city was now shorthand for a certain music occurred during a vacation to St. Louis in 1992. A band poster on a telephone poll I saw listed three bands I'd never heard of. That shouldn't be surprising, given that this was miles from my hometown, but it was the word "Seattle" that drew my eye in the first place. Atop the poster was a banner headline, ten times bigger than the band names, that read FROM SEATTLE.

It seemed absurd to me that three unknown bands could tour the Midwest as long as they made their home address bigger on a poster than their names. In early 1992, even Kurt Cobain couldn't legitimately put "From Seattle" on a Nirvana poster, but in the public's mind that little detail hardly mattered. He was "Seattle's Kurt Cobain" already, and would remain so.

FIVE

HAPPENS EVERY DAY
Addiction & Suicide

Kurt Cobain was not just one of the most influential musicians of his generation; he was also one of the era's most famous drug addicts. Kurt experienced great fame, of course, but drug addiction is an undeniable part of that fame, and of his legacy. His death, however horrible, has had an undeniable effect on how musicians are now treated for addiction, and on how managers and record labels respond to clients who struggle with drugs. In the fields of thanatology, the science of death, and suicidology, the science of suicide, Kurt's life and death have been widely analyzed, investigated, and written about.

For all the identification Kurt would have as a heroin

addict in the eyes of the public, that phase of his life came fairly late. For his first twenty-four years, Kurt Cobain was not a drug addict, and was often the most sober of his group of friends. When his heroin addiction began, it came as a great shock to some friends: Kurt was so afraid of needles that he once ran out of a doctor's office when a physician tried to give him a shot. Once, in his early adulthood, Kurt attended a Halloween party dressed in a junkie costume, complete with fake track marks drawn on his arms. Kurt's thin frame was already what many imagined a drug addict to look like, and rumors of his drug use began to plague him around 1990 in Olympia, in part because of that Halloween costume. Two years later, it was true.

Up until 1991, Kurt also rarely drank to excess, as he always worried about his constant stomach problems. He did occasionally take pills, and he smoked marijuana, but he was too poor to afford to do any drug regularly. He was prone to trying new diets, both to bulk up and to try to help fix his stomach issues, and for several different stints, sometimes as long as six months, he would go on regimens in which he would not drink or smoke at all. On one of Nirvana's first tours, Kurt was the most health-conscious member of the band and complained about the other guys partying too much, which he felt took away from the serious task of music making. He would not stay the most health-conscious band member, however.

His use of heroin began in 1991, and that occasional use became an addiction by the end of the year. He wrote in his journal that he "made a decision" to become a heroin addict, something he romanticized at first, going so far as to describe the drug as "heroine" when he wrote about it, and he was well aware of the sarcasm of that. Most of Kurt's initial motivation to use came from his discovery that heroin relieved his stomach pain. Kurt did not initially seek heroin out—as with many, a friend introduced him to the drug—but soon he was the one among his group of friends who would suggest getting high. He used more and more, though his pitiful financial state initially worked as a governor, to limit his addiction. But fame brought money, and money brought heroin. What began as a way to seek relief from his stomach pain turned into an addiction that caused withdrawal pain anytime he tried to quit or go a single day without the drug. Pain relief begot pain.

Soon, though, Kurt's romanticism about heroin addiction disappeared and his journal became the most strident anti-drug message you could ever read. As he lost his freedom

to his addiction, and as it had increasingly negative consequences for him, he often begged God to free him from the
addiction—but those prayers were not answered. He did attempt to use willpower to break his habit, but without much
success. He attended twelve-step meetings during a couple
of phases, but pronounced them not right for him. Judge his
initial choice to pursue drugs if you will, but Kurt did spend
at least five separate stints in rehabilitation centers or private
doctor clinics, attempting to kick heroin. None of those stints
went on long enough to be truly successful, but that he attempted to get clean so many times shows how desperate he
was to stop.

His drug use did not remain a secret to the general public
for long. In an interview with a journalist in 1992, he nodded
off, a telltale sign of drug use, and this was reported in the
press. From that point on, Kurt lived under a shadow both in
the media and with the public. That shame or watchfulness
didn't stop him from doing drugs, but in his later interviews
he consistently claimed that addiction was in his past. He used
language about how he had "been" an addict, and he consistently downplayed his usage. "I did heroin for three weeks
[at the start of 1992]," he said in an interview with the *Los
Angeles Times* in the fall of that year. When he put his drug

use so far in his past, he made it sound as if he was a changed man who had come to his senses. This was his own projection; this was Kurt imagining the man he wanted to be. But then in the next interview, the timeline of his "past" drug use would change. There never was enough time being sober to even create a "past" history and "current" sobriety. Kurt was always in current addiction.

There was a point when I was working on *Heavier Than Heaven* when I tried to create a timeline for Kurt's drug addiction, charting out his overdoses and his stints in rehab and pairing them with when he said in interviews he was sober. The math simply did not add up. He'd talk in these interviews about having several weeks free from drugs, but friends told of him consistently using, and police and medical records proved that point. At one point I even called up Courtney Love and posed the question to her. I told her that in the window of the last eighteen months of Kurt's life—when his addiction was most extreme—I simply couldn't find a full week when he was sober, much less the several weeks he kept referring to in progressive interviews with magazines. Courtney's response was one word, but it proved how much I still didn't understand of the depths of Kurt's struggles. "Duh," she said. And then she continued, "He was an addict. What did you think?"

I had wanted—like every biographer who wishes the best for his subject—for the story to have been prettier, for drugs not to have had such a stranglehold over him. At best, I wanted a better life for Kurt, but at worst, I was naïve.

As Kurt's life went on, the addiction became worse and worse. There were more overdoses, suicide attempts, arrests, and all of it going on while he was still the biggest rock star in the world. Anything he did was news then; anything controversial he and Courtney did together was even bigger news. They kept making headlines even though their lives kept getting smaller, caught up in a spiral of addiction where Kurt wouldn't leave the house for days, sometimes weeks.

Many people outside their world wanted to blame Courtney for Kurt's addiction, but even several of Kurt's closest friends who had an intense dislike of Courtney were adamant that this wasn't the case. Two addicts holed together in a nest with money and drugs was never a good situation, but she most certainly did not get him "hooked on drugs" in the first place, as is often believed. Kurt was into heroin well before Courtney's arrival. Kurt's three girlfriends prior to Courtney all told stories about how his experimentation with drugs drove him away from them. And in Kurt's marriage to Courtney, there were a number of times when his behavior was more reprehensible than hers. Courtney went through more periods of sobriety than Kurt, and during one of those she even attended twelve-step meetings. Kurt knew when Courtney was sober, and he often would be in the next room using even though his wife had just come from a meeting of narcotics users trying to stay clean. But in a marriage that included two drug users, it makes little difference which addict was worse or better at any given moment. One of their closest friends put it to me this way: they were like two characters in a play, the perpetrator and the victim, the addict and the nagging spouse, and they switched roles daily, sometimes hourly. Whether she was a good or bad choice as a mate in the eyes of the rest of the world didn't matter to Kurt. Reading their correspondence and his diaries it was clear to me that he picked her just as much as she picked him.

When Kurt died in 1994, his drug use got another, more extensive examination in the court of public opinion. His death was big news and had the effect of scaring straight some of the drug addicts I knew in the Seattle music scene. But it certainly didn't stop drug use, in Seattle or anywhere else. The weekend after Kurt's death, many of Kurt's Seattle friends drank or drugged themselves to oblivion, trying to escape the shock and pain. Kurt and I had mutual friends, and one who had been sober for a few months fell back into the darkness that week. Kurt's death made many who knew him feel hopeless. That particular friend died a few years ago, the final few years of abuse killing him in what was, in a way, a slow suicide. That story was repeated again and again.

Eventually, though, Kurt's tragic death made many in the music industry, particularly treatment professionals and musicians, rethink addiction. Over the years, I've met at least a dozen A-list musicians who told me privately—when the tape recorder was off—that seeing the stark reality of addiction so laid out in Kurt's life made them change their ways. There is a line in twelve-step literature that says the only outcome of untreated addiction is "jails, institutions, and death." Kurt hit all three, and never was there a life where the ultimate price of addiction was as clearly spelled out. If nothing else, his life has served as a cautionary tale.

"I didn't stop immediately after he died," one musician told me once. "But seeing what happened to Kurt, I had to look at things. It took a year, but I got help."

Since Kurt's death, more attention by mental health researchers has been placed on how drug and alcohol abuse are involved with suicide—several studies show that as many as two thirds of suicides involve substance abuse in some form. "Since Kurt's death, treatment for alcohol or drug addiction has changed drastically, as we now are delving into the under-lying causes and condition of the entire addictive disease pro-cess," says Erica Krusen of MusiCares. "Once, treatment fa-cilities may have focused primarily on intervention or detox, but they are now learning to assess and identify co-occurring psychiatric conditions, such as major depression and/or anxi-ety that, left unaddressed, will likely result in repeated relapses or risk for suicide."

MusiCares is a charitable wing of the organization that gives out the Grammy Awards, and they provide anonymous treatment options for musicians battling addiction. The group has raised millions for treatment through benefit concerts fea-turing the likes of Paul McCartney, Neil Young, Carole King, and Bruce Springsteen. MusiCares has helped thousands of musicians get treatment and resources to stay sober. It has also helped—anonymously of course—several Seattle musicians who knew Kurt, and a few who even did drugs with him. In the early nineties, some of these resources were not available to musicians, or at least not widely known of.

Harold Owens is the senior director of MusiCares, but he

was also previously a counselor in the very drug-treatment clinic Kurt last attended, and worked on the same ward that Kurt was assigned to. Owens says Kurt's death was a "wake-up call" to the music community and made managers and record labels specifically rethink their roles. Even as horrible as Kurt's death was, Owens says many musicians sought treatment because of it, and continue to do so. "A lot of people got sober as a result, maybe not then, but a seed was planted that they could get help," he told me.

Band managers began to look at addiction on a monetary level, realizing that early death means the end of a business revenue stream and, strictly from a financial standpoint, requires quicker action than previously thought. Drug addiction is now thought of as an occupational hazard. Bands take "sober coaches" on the road, and some bands create no-alcohol zones backstage. At every major festival or music-industry event, private twelve-step groups are organized to provide support; MusiCares hands out business cards listing a toll-free treatment line, and the cards are routinely posted backstage at many venues, or in bathrooms and dressing rooms, so that musicians in need will know where to find help if they seek it.

But the biggest change in the past twenty years is in attitude. "Before the nineties," Owen says, "there was a myth that there was no way out, that getting sober would also mean losing creativity. But since Kurt's death, a lot of well-known people have gotten sober, and the myths have dissipated."

Kurt's death even moved some in his family to speak publicly about the impact of addiction and suicide on the family unit. His aunt Beverly Cobain has written two books on preventing and coping with suicide, including *Dying to Be Free: A Healing Guide for Families After a Suicide*. Kurt's favorite and closest aunt, Mari Earle, was also inspired to create a presentation on drug addiction that she gives in high schools. She has talked to thousands of teens. Hearing about Kurt's struggles from one of his closest relatives gives a face to the battle with addiction, making it seem more personal than an episode of *Celebrity Rehab*.

There was no *Celebrity Rehab* in Kurt's era. He most certainly would never have gone on that program, as he felt so much shame from both his addiction and his fame. But two decades after his death it seems that celebrities of all ages and levels of fame can take to the airwaves and announce that they are seeking treatment for addiction. As a public, we barely bat an eye now. Tragedies involving drug addiction and suicide continue, but the idea that celebrities can openly discuss their struggles is a given today.

Any fight with addiction is a difficult battle in which success is measured in days clean, and in which the language of recovery speaks of "a daily reprieve" rather than a cure. Four of Kurt's friends I interviewed for *Heavier Than Heaven* have since died of drug-related causes in the last decade. But several other close friends of Kurt's—all horribly addicted at one point, one severely enough that I thought his body was the one that had been discovered at Kurt's home—remain sober.

It feels awful to even write these words, but Kurt is better known now for his suicide than for anything else. Even those who know nothing about Nirvana, or music, or Kurt's personal artistry know he took his own life in April 1994 with a shotgun. He is one of the most famous people to ever commit suicide. Any search for suicide on the Internet immediately yields Kurt's name near the top, along with Sylvia Plath, Vincent Van Gogh, and Hunter S. Thompson.

Kurt's suicide made front-page news around the world, made the cover of many magazines (*Newsweek*'s headline read: SUICIDE: WHY DO PEOPLE KILL THEMSELVES?), was reported on every major television news broadcast, was the subject of round-the-clock coverage on MTV, and was the topic of days of discussions on talk radio. "Kurt became synonymous with suicide," says therapist Nicole Jon Carroll. For a time his suicide so dominated public thought it "removed him from the brilliance of his artistry," she says. Carroll would know firsthand: in addition to being a noted therapist, she was Kurt's sister-in-law.

Kurt's suicide affected the lives of his family and his fans, but it was not a unique story—except for the fact that he was famous. That same year, in 1994, 30,574 other people killed themselves in the United States. Suicide has become such a public health issue that combating it is now the responsibility of the Centers for Disease Control and Prevention (CDC), as if it were the plague or the Ebola virus. The CDC estimates that for every actual suicide there are eleven unsuccessful attempts, meaning that in the year of Kurt's death, several hundred thousand Americans tried to take their own lives. Worldwide, the numbers are in the millions.

Even those closest to Kurt, and who suffered the greatest loss, realized his death was one of many. "It's not uncommon what happened with Kurt," Krist Novoselic told me once. "The same story happens all over this country every day. It's a combination of drug abuse and lack of coping skills."

The Washington State Youth Suicide Prevention Plan,

which was instituted the year after Kurt's death, identifies the major risk factors for suicide. They read like Kurt's résumé: previous suicide attempt (Kurt made at least half a dozen attempts); past or current psychiatric disorder (like depression); alcohol and/or drug abuse (severe for Kurt); access to firearms (Kurt had many weapons). One other risk factor not on that list, but that experts agree plays a role, is a family history of suicide. There is much thought in scientific circles that researchers will find a "suicide gene." A 2002 study published in the academic journal *Archives of General Psychiatry* found that children whose parents had attempted suicide were six times more likely to attempt suicide themselves. Some of the public discourse on this was reignited in 2009 when Nicholas Hughes, the son of Sylvia Plath and one of her two children in the house when she committed suicide, took his own life at forty-seven.

Kurt's family history of suicide was significant. Two of his uncles took their own lives, and his great-grandfather committed suicide in front of his family. There was also a family history of depression and alcohol abuse, and many in the field feel there is a strong genetic component to depression and addiction. Researchers continue to look for a suicide gene, but what is known is that certain regions have significantly higher suicide rates. Social scientists think that when suicide is common in one area, and this greatest of all human taboos is crossed, it gives vulnerable people "permission" when a period of suicidal thought hits. In Kurt's case, he had so much suicide in his family and in his hometown, he was already talking about taking his own life as a young teen. Kurt came upon a suicide victim himself when he was in middle school, discovering a man who had hanged himself in a tree. That vision was most certainly indelible in Kurt's young brain—he extensively talked about it with his childhood friends—and the sheer happenstance of that discovery became yet another horrific part of his history.

I often see things written along the lines of "Kurt Cobain killed himself because of fame." Maybe. But consider that before Kurt ever picked up a guitar he had seen a suicide victim hanging from a tree, he had family members on both sides of his lineage who had chosen suicide, he had family histories of depression and alcohol abuse, and he grew up in an economically depressed area where unemployment and suicide rates were high. It is possible that before he ever picked up a guitar, he didn't have a chance. It is possible that fame, rather than taking his life, perhaps gave him more years than he would have had without it. What we do know for certain is that growing up knowing other family members have committed suicide, as was the case for Kurt, increases risk significantly.

The sad story of suicide in our society has continued since Kurt's death. In the two decades since, suicide rates in the United States have steadily increased, according the CDC. In 2010, 38,354 people committed suicide in the US. Thirty-three percent tested positive for alcohol, 23 percent for antidepressants, and 20 percent for opiates. In a given year in America, suicide results in an estimated $34.6 billion in medical costs and work lost. Though young females attempt suicide at a greater rate than men, more men die from suicide since they are more likely to be successful in their attempt—what suicide researchers called the gender paradox. Young men are particularly vulnerable, and according to Suicide.org there are four male deaths by suicide for every female suicide death. Suicide is the second leading cause of death for adults of either gender twenty-seven years of age, after only car accidents. Kurt turned twenty-seven in February 1994.

It truly does happen every day.

Initially, however, Kurt's widely reported death caused great alarm among public health officials, who feared it was the perfect storm to threaten vulnerable youth. Celebrity suicides have been known to cause copycats, or "suicide clusters." When Marilyn Monroe died in 1962, her suicide was extensively studied because she was such a high-profile celebrity with passionate fans. The following month there were two hundred more suicides than usual in the United States. Given Kurt's large fan base among an age group already at risk, a catastrophe was feared after his death.

Immediately after Kurt's death, every suicide or suicide attempt in the Seattle area was examined for potential linkages by researchers. One young man did go home after Kurt's public memorial service and take his own life, and that suicide was widely reported in the press, with speculation that it could be the first of a wave.

There are many websites devoted to Kurt conspiracy theories, suggesting that he did not take his own life; a few of these sites also record copycat suicides. These sites argue that the "crime" of Kurt's supposed murder is all the more heinous and tragic because it resulted in the deaths of further innocent victims. One of these conspiracy websites lists nineteen "Cobain-related sympathetic 'copycat' suicides"; another says there are "at least sixty-eight." Their salacious reports have received widespread media attention.

But what has not gotten as much exposure is the science and detailed statistical analysis by public health experts after Kurt's suicide. Remarkably, the statistics in King County, where Kurt lived and died, show that the number of suicides actually went down in the months following Kurt's death. It wasn't a huge decrease, but it was significant given generally rising suicide rates. Moreover, the fact that there wasn't a huge spike was the opposite of what researchers expected, the opposite of what has been reported numerous times in the media, and is in stark conflict to what has been claimed countless times on those conspiracy websites.

Dr. David A. Jobes is a leading suicide expert and the author of one of those studies done after Kurt's death. He says the figures on the decrease in suicides in the wake of Kurt's death initially surprised him, but they've been confirmed by several further analyses. Another extensive study showed suicides went down significantly right after his death, even in places as far from Seattle as Australia, where Kurt was beloved.

I was in my office when news of Kurt's suicide came to me with that phone call, but Jobes had perhaps an even more surreal experience learning about it. He was actually attending an international convention of suicide researchers that week; he heard the news sitting in a bar discussing trends in the field when a breaking news report came across the television in the background. "It was the headline story," Jobes told me, "and I was with a guy from the CDC, and our jaws just dropped. 'This is going to be bad,' we said. We thought there was going to be an epidemic."

Jobes's extensive study found the opposite occurred. The paper he published speculates several reasons: "The lack of an apparent copycat effect in Seattle may be due to various aspects of the media coverage, the method used in Cobain's suicide, and the crisis center and community outreach interventions that occurred." Jobes says another key was outreach by the medical community in the previous year to establish a protocol for suicide coverage, urging media outlets to include suicide resources in their reports. Kurt's death "was the first time where articles appeared with little boxes that listed hotline numbers, signs of depression, and places to get help," Jobes said. He says Kurt's death was something of an "outlier of a celebrity suicide in that it arguably led to reporting that did some good."

Vicki Wagner, executive director of Seattle's Youth Suicide Prevention Program, says Kurt's death still has a role in raising awareness two decades later. "It made young adults, and certainly teens, much more open to talking about suicide, and normalizing it, even if it's a topic that is never really normalized," she says. "His death made kids look at the reality of what the impact of your suicide would be."

In Jobes's study, his researchers actually went into the homes of people who took their lives after Kurt's death and searched for Nirvana CDs and posters and examined notes for linkages. Statistically, when a band sells thirty-five million CDs, their music will likely show up on the shelves of some of those who will take their lives, but Jobes and other researchers looked beyond that. What they found demonstrated that Nirvana fans did not kill themselves simply because of his death. "The results were what we call a 'proactive non-varietor effect,'" Jobes says, meaning that the attention and circumstances of Kurt's death may have actually encouraged people to seek help: his research concluded that Kurt's death statistically decreased suicides among Nirvana fans in the period studied. In some strange way, Kurt dying may have saved lives.

Of all the field notes that Jobes reported in his extensive research, none was more eerie to read about than the case of one young Nirvana fan who did attempt, and succeeded, at taking her own life just a week after Kurt's death. She had been well aware of resources that the media reported were available, but in her final note to the world she wrote that she couldn't make use of that help. But she also made a remarkable revelation in her suicide note—she wrote that although she loved Kurt, she was taking her life not because he had, but because of her own issues and depression. "In her note," Jobes says, "she said she wanted to 'own' her own suicide, and didn't want it linked to his. Some went into this believing an ecological fallacy," Jobes says—the assumption that people who killed themselves after the death of a celebrity did so because of that news story. In the instance of Kurt Cobain's suicide, science does not back up that assumption, and in fact the opposite was true.

Exactly why a person chooses suicide is an inexact science. The only subject who can definitively explain his motivation is dead. Still, Jobes speculates several key factors that played a part in minimizing copycats and lowering the suicide rate following Cobain's. One was Kurt's chosen method of death, which alone diminished copycats because of the intense violence involved. The thought of pain can halt suicidal impulsivity, and while this may seem counterintuitive, it's a correlation suicide researchers find often: it's also why sharp spikes under a bridge can halt suicides at that location. Though media coverage of Kurt's death had lurid moments, the fact that Kurt's method of suicide was widely reported in detail made it less romantic to young fans. The Seattle mayor's office and governmental offices in other cities also put out press releases that gave contacts for resources, another critical part of the response.

Another key element Jobes cites as a suicide-deterrent factor was Seattle's public memorial for Kurt. It drew thousands to Seattle Center on Sunday, April 10, 1994, just two days after Kurt's body was discovered. It was one of the most extraordinary events I've ever witnessed.

Immediately after the news of Kurt's death was disclosed on Friday, fans gathered at the public park that was next to his home in Seattle's Denny-Blaine neighborhood. I drove there myself when I finally got out of my office that nightmare day. I saw fans weeping, holding candles, or propping photographs of Kurt against the park benches. As at many of the events that were related to Kurt and Grunge, I had dual roles: I was a fan myself, and grieving, but I was also a journalist. Looking at the greenhouse where he'd been discovered, I still couldn't believe he'd been alive in that room not long ago, but now the whole place was covered in yellow police tape. We would later learn, when the medical examiner determined Kurt most likely died on April 5, that his corpse had lain undiscovered in that greenhouse for three days.

It became obvious that a larger public Seattle memorial needed to happen. The Seattle music community quickly organized a vigil and scheduled it for Sunday the tenth at Seattle Center's fountain pavilion. Several radio stations helped spread the word and agreed to broadcast it. Though the main purpose was to honor Kurt, there was also some subterfuge in the planning: it was scheduled to run at the same time as the private funeral. There had been some fear that fans would swamp the funeral, which was to be an invitation-only affair. Press were also barred from the funeral, even local press, even newspapers Kurt used to pay twenty dollars to advertise in.

When I walked onto the Seattle Center grounds that Sunday, I expected a crowd, and the seventy-four-acre public park was filled with Nirvana fans. Police estimated seven thousand were in attendance, but there could have been many more, as there were pockets of fans for blocks around Seattle Center, sitting in circles, playing guitar, lighting candles, holding pictures. At the memorial, a small stage platform was set up with speakers, and I went behind it, ran into Marco Collins, and asked him what exactly was going to happen. "I don't really know, and I'm one of the organizers," he said. "A few people will talk, and we are going to play this tape Courtney made."

Marco said a few words when the event started, and so did a couple of other DJs. Then a short recording by Krist Novoselic was played that urged fans to find their own muse, follow Kurt's punk-rock ethic, and never forget that "no band is special, no player royalty." Next was Courtney's tape. She began by announcing she was recording it in their bed. The crowd was completely silent as she spoke. I have never been in a crowd of seven thousand and had them be that quiet— never. The recording was so clear you could hear Courtney taking a drag off her cigarette. She said was going to read Kurt's suicide note. "Some of it is to you," she said, referring to Kurt's fans. But before reading it, she asked the crowd to yell " 'asshole' really loud." And they yelled it. It was kind of a loud communal wail of anger, pain, sadness. Then, for the next fifteen minutes, Courtney herself wailed, screamed, and read virtually every line of Kurt's suicide note.

If the idea for the memorial had begun as subterfuge to keep the masses away from the nearby private funeral, it turned into the most amazing spectacle of public grief I've ever witnessed or been a part of. Not long after her recording was over, when the private funeral ended, Courtney even showed up at Seattle Center. She was holding Kurt's suicide note. She sat with groups of fans and let them hold and read Kurt's note. Shakespeare never wrote such drama for the stage.

But the entire event, more through happenstance than planning, turned into brilliant public health policy. Because Courtney, and the media, specifically addressed how Kurt died, Jobes thinks the public memorial at Seattle Center was the absolute turning point. Courtney spoke very specifically about what Kurt did to himself, which Jobes says took away any glamour that might have been associated with the act and showed how much pain was left for others after his suicide. "It was really powerful for her to read that note, with all her rage," Jobes says, "because it punched a hole into the romantic expectation of suicide." After Love's recording was played, a suicide-prevention expert talked to the crowd, offering options and information on how to seek help. In the end, Jobes says, "it was a disaster averted."

Jobes has studied suicide for years, and as it grows as a cause of death, he says education, rather than a moral reaction, is key. Particularly within rock music, he says, Tipper Gore's attacks on violent lyrics were completely misguided given what science has found: "We've done three different studies on suicidal rock music lyrics, things like Pearl Jam's 'Jeremy.'" While fans of these songs may show increased suicidal thoughts, their exposure to what Jobes calls a "prosocial response" actually decreases their suicide rate. In other words, being sad and listening to a song about sadness helps you feel better, not worse, and rock music doesn't lead you to kill yourself.

Jobes has also extensively researched suicide notes. Kurt's, he reports, unfortunately fits into a pattern that is all too common, what researchers call "the perceived burdensomeness syndrome." It means that suicidal people believe that those around them will be better off with them gone. "A person convinces themselves they are not only ending their own suffering, they are giving the people they love a gift," Jobes says. "They misperceive."

In his years as a researcher, Jobes has also researched the impact of suicide on the families left behind. The greatest tragedy of the "perceived burdensomeness syndrome," he says, is that those left—those families, those friends, those music fans—are "never better off."

I knew very little about suicide or heroin addiction before I began to write about Kurt's life, and I'll admit I approached his history with judgments. To face my own preconceptions, I was forced to confront my biases and to educate myself, particularly about drug addiction.

I came from a family burdened by alcoholism. There were more than a few parallels in my own story to Kurt's: we were both from divorced families; we both grew up in small towns in Washington State, isolated from the larger city; and we both turned to the arts, to a degree, because we didn't fit in on the football team. In my own internal emotional life I knew darkness, too. Still, no matter how strained my childhood had been, it hadn't led to heroin addiction. Therefore I thought of heroin addiction—as do many in society—as the worst of the worst, the lowest moral choice.

But as I began to study drug addiction, I saw that any judgments, good or bad, didn't solve the problem. Many of our laws about drugs are based on making those sitting on high moral ground feel superior about their own choices, but they don't solve our public health crisis. That's where my beliefs have moved now: that the our current punishment-based drug policies only cost us more in resources, without treating addiction as the disease it is.

My feelings shifted for several reasons, but in part because of a public health official who worked for King County. This woman spent a considerable amount of time helping me understand the face of drug addiction in Seattle, where an estimated ten thousand opiate addicts live. Statistically Seattle, like many port cities, has always had a higher incidence of heroin use than other locales. Seattle is also on the West Coast corridor where the heroin trade is controlled by Mexican drug cartels. The cartels are adept at distribution, and as a result their brand of heroin, black tar, is cheap and plentiful. It also represents a type of heroin that leaves users—Kurt included—particularly susceptible to secondary infections from the many agents used to cut it. Though figures on the exact size of addict populations are difficult to compile, in the twenty years since Kurt's death, things have only gotten worse in Seattle, according to the Drug Enforcement Administration. In 2013, the DEA called heroin Seattle's "public enemy number one" due to an increased number of busts, ninety-eight local overdose deaths in 2012, and a rising crossover from prescription drug addicts switching to heroin because it's cheaper.

That health worker who filled me in on heroin addiction explained in great detail what using the drug entailed in terms of acquiring and injecting it and its long-term physical and health consequences. I needed to understand these things, to understand what the fabric of life meant for Kurt. There are an estimated ten thousand opiate addicts in Seattle. Those thousands of addicts have to figure out, every day, how to buy, use, and finance their addictions. Some of them steal stereos, but many support their addiction with jobs, as Kurt did. One of the professions where drug addiction is highest is among medical workers—nurses, doctors—because they work in high-stress environments and have easy access to drugs. These aren't down-and-out street people, but rather professionals with lives and families. Addiction crosses all economic barriers, genders, ethnicities, and neighborhoods.

I learned what Narcan was, why people around Kurt always had a supply of this overdose-prevention drug, and that Washington State is one of the few where it is legal to possess it without a prescription. In many other localities, just carrying Narcan, which has no use other than saving the life of someone overdosing, is illegal. I learned that while I'd always thought overdose was the biggest heroin health risk, there were many other deadly infections possible from the black tar heroin sold in Seattle. I learned that hepatitis C will soon kill more people than AIDS and cost our nation billions to treat. I later discovered that many of the friends Kurt used heroin with have hep C now, and that he almost certainly had it, too.

All of this opened my eyes, but the next stop in my heroin-education tour also had an effect. It was important that I research the physiological effects of overdose to understand two key pieces of Kurt's history: why he didn't die from numerous overdoses, and how he was able to take a large amount of heroin on his final day, and still take his own life with a gun. Needless to say, these were not assignments I thought would ever be in my appointment book when I was in journalism school. The second point was critical, however, because most of the conspiracy theories on Kurt's death—there is a industry of them with books, websites, and a supposed "nonfiction" film—begin with the concept that Kurt was so high there would be no way he could have taken his own life.

To believe there was a conspiracy, you would first have to believe that the two dozen Seattle police who filtered through this high-profile case were all—every one—somehow in ca-hoots in a cover-up when they concluded beyond any doubt that it was a suicide. I have since come to know that if some-one wants to believe a conspiracy theory, though, the more factual data you present, the more their paranoia increases and their doubt grows. Like a Whac-A-Mole game at the arcade, no matter how much you beat them down, they spring back renewed. Presidential historian Robert Dallek was recently quoted in *The New York Times* suggesting that the reason so many can't accept that Oswald killed Kennedy is because to do so "shows people how random the world is, how uncer-tain. I think it pains them; they don't want to accept that fact." With Kurt's fans, I think something else is at play, too: if they can blame someone else, anyone else, for Kurt's choices, then they can see him forever as an innocent victim, and that makes them feel less betrayed by his actions.

Yet to accept that the entire Seattle Police Department was in on a "fraud," you must also accept that Dr. Nikolas Hartshorne was in on a "fraud," too. Dr. Hartshorne was the King County medical examiner who worked on the investi-gation and conducted Kurt's autopsy. I knew who Dr. Hart-shorne was—he'd been the longtime boyfriend of a person I worked with at *The Rocket*. He was a brilliant doctor who cared very much that Kurt's investigation be handled carefully and methodically. His words to me were that if anything whatsoever had been suspicious in the circumstances of Kurt's death, he would have "gone to the end of the earth to investigate it." And Kurt's death, Dr. Hartshorne told me, was, without a doubt, suicide. He also leaked me documents and information related to Kurt's death as I was doing research because he wanted to make sure I knew every aspect of how it was investigated.

Dr. Hartshorne died a year after *Heavier Than Heaven* came out. He was a base jumper, leaping from the sides of mountains as a hobby when he wasn't excelling in his professional life. There is so much conspiracy hubbub on the Internet about Kurt's death that it disturbs me, but nothing offends me more than reading that Dr. Hartshorne's death is yet another part in "the chain" of the "massive cover-up." Dr. Hartshorne had completed 501 successful base jumps and, apparently, we are to believe that on the 502nd jump the conspiracy rolled in, blew the wind in a new direction, and took his life.

But back before Dr. Hartshorne died, I questioned him several times about why the toxicology report showed a level of heroin that might have been fatal for others but didn't kill Kurt. He told me that longtime hard-core addicts can build a tolerance that creates a wide variance on what a lethal dose is, or how long it would take for such a dose to cause the onset of death. He also referred me to experts who were meeting in Seattle that next week for the annual international convention—imagine this—of public health workers trying to prevent heroin overdose.

I attended that convention. I asked many of the world's experts these questions, and they confirmed what Dr. Hartshorne had told me. One medical examiner told me there was a case of a man who had taken twice the heroin Kurt did and was still able to ride a bicycle in a laboratory. A dose of heroin that might kill a normal person wouldn't necessarily cause the death of a serious addict. This one particularly awful piece of science also helps explain many rock 'n' roll relapse deaths. Addicts gets clean for a long period of time, get the drug out of their system, and then relapse and use the same dose they previously used during their addiction—which is now fatal. But Kurt never got clean enough to lower his tolerance.

At that overdose convention, I saw a presentation that did more to change my attitudes and moral judgments about drug addiction, and the world's approach to solving it, than anything else. A man took the stage and began a ten-minute slide show that started with photos of babies, then Boy Scouts, cheerleaders, two kids at a prom. It went on to show grad-uation photos, weddings, and families. As I watched, I had no idea what linked these people of different ages, races, and genders. It froze on a photo of a beautiful young girl, and the man stepped to the front of the stage and spoke. "Every person you've just seen was loved, had a family, a father, a mother, friends, some had sons, some had daughters, and all had dreams," he said. "And everyone you just saw was someone who died in the last calendar year of an overdose of heroin, including this last one, my daughter Megan. Most of these deaths could have been prevented if we stopped looking at drug use as a moral problem and began looking at ways we can save lives with public health decisions based on science." By the time the man was done talking, there wasn't a dry eye in the house, even among these scientists.

The man was from Australia, and part of his presentation was how harm-reduction centers there—clinics where addicts can use drugs with medical supervision—had lowered over-dose deaths, cut down on transmission rates of AIDS and hep-atitis C, and given officials access to addicts so they could get treatment information into their hands, none of which is pos-sible when someone is using in an alley. His daughter had, un-fortunately, not been in a city where such a clinic was available.

"We are not going to save a single life until we stop our moral judgments about heroin addiction," he said. "We need to start finding solutions based in science, based on policies that work, based on harm reduction, and not based on moralism."

Kurt Cobain's photograph did not appear among those that passed by during the slide show—this was a few years after his death. Several, though, were of slight, blond-haired, blue-eyed boys. They looked almost exactly like him.

SIX

THE LAST ROCK STAR
Legacy & Blue Eyes

In many ways, Kurt Cobain was the last rock star. I don't mean that to diminish the numerous other great musical talents of the last twenty years, but there has not been any single performer in rock 'n' roll since with Kurt's combination of raw talent, charisma, ambition, and, most important, songwriting genius. There are dozens of bands that have produced classic albums, and Adele, for example, is a superstar of immense talent and voice. But Kurt had both a certain kind of rock-star bearing and a lyrical gift, and rarely are the two combined. Kurt also had a darkness that was a key element of his lyrical gift. Krist Novoselic once told me that to understand Kurt you had to understand that there was also something wrong with him, something abnormal, and it was one of the keys to his artistry. "The music was this dark, angry, beautiful, rageful thing," Krist told me. "It had beauty, but there was something not quite right about it. It was kind of disturbed. That's what separated him from all the other people of the era—he was an artist, and they weren't."

When Kurt died twenty years ago, I expected there would be many stars who would come along and vault onto the list of the all-time greats, maybe leapfrogging Kurt. For a variety of reasons, that hasn't happened, but that dearth also magnifies Kurt's place in history and plays a role in his legacy. His death, however tragic and ill-timed for a thousand reasons, was good timing in one particular way: he exists on a spot on the timeline of rock 'n' roll greats, just before the last punctuation point.

This may be in part because Kurt died at the start of so many major shifts in the music industry, just as technology was transforming the entire world. It's not just that Kurt Cobain overshadowed his peers and those who came after, but that the very playing field has changed. The last twenty years in the music industry, with the advent of MP3s, downloading, and streaming, have represented a rapid shift in the way people buy and experience music. *Nevermind* is one of the last rock records to end up in the collection of nearly everyone a certain age, bought as a cohesive whole—as an album, which now seems like a radical concept itself—in record stores. Today most music is sold electronically, it's sold as songs mostly, and total music album sales are now a fraction of what they were two decades ago. Only one rock band made it to the top-ten album sales chart for 2012, and that was Mumford and Sons, who sold 1.5 million copies of *Babel*—compare that to *Nevermind*, which sold ten million copies in just one watershed year. *Nevermind*'s impact, both commercially and artistically, would have been significantly diminished if fans had been able to purchase a few tracks on iTunes and skip buying the entire album. Genres of music are fractionalized now to the degree that the same rock record blasting from every radio station seems an impossibility. Had his career launched ten years later, Kurt's kind of fame, which combined celebrity and artistry, probably wouldn't have happened. In today's YouTube era, when sudden fame comes as much for being outrageous as it does for the quality of the songs a musician crafts, Kurt would have been adrift.

Kurt was not of these modern times. Most of Kurt's own music collection was on cassette tapes, some of them recorded off the radio after waiting for the perfect song to come on, then trying to hit the record button at just the right moment. He spent months of his life in his crappy little apartment watching hours of MTV, trying to record a clip of a video onto his VCR or waiting to just watch something by his favorite band of the moment. To even find music in his youth, Kurt had to dig through musty bins of vinyl albums in record stores, looking for one particular album that seemed impossible to find, or he had to borrow an album from a friend. He drove all the way to Seattle once when he was a young teen to search for an album he'd heard on the radio and looked through several second-hand stores until he finally located it: it was an REO Speed-wagon record that just a few years later he would have been incredibly embarrassed to have owned. In all these instances, Kurt had to interact with other humans, record-store clerks, or his buddies to buy or borrow records, which created a sense of community. Kurt couldn't go to Amazon and download a song instantly—he had to search the physical world. And in the physical world, he found lasting connections. He'd first met Krist Novoselic in high school, but their friendship—the most lasting musical connection of Kurt's life—was formed when Kurt went into the Aberdeen Burger King, where Novoselic worked, to drop off a cassette tape for Krist. An online transfer of MP3s would not have created that one momentous meeting, the casual conversation ("Hey, what kind of music do you like?"), the eye-to-eye connection, and the lifetime friendship that ensued and went on to create Nirvana.

Kurt was a rock star in an era when everything in music took time and effort. When Nirvana needed to find a new drummer, Kurt drove an hour to *The Rocket* office, placed a classified ad, and then waited weeks for interested parties to mail him a letter. Making a record was so expensive, with pressing costs and studio fees, that Kurt had to find a record label to help, which required him to write hundreds of letters to labels. Every one rejected him. When Nirvana's first single, "Love Buzz," was finally pressed by Sub Pop, Kurt took that physical 45-RPM single in hand to Seattle radio station KCMU, drove to a phone booth afterward, used a quarter to dial the station to request his own song, and then sat in his car for a very long time waiting to hear it played. That same radio station is now KEXP, an Internet pioneer with vast numbers of listeners worldwide, where requests can be made on a website and any performance that happened in the station's studio can be found on YouTube or in an online archive and heard anytime. That's an entirely different universe from the one where Kurt, or I, came of age.

There was something about that earlier, slower time in history that helped make Kurt who he was. He owned only a couple hundred records, so it was a small sampling. In that pre-Internet world, he discovered and listened to many of these records on his own, or after reading clips in magazines or fanzines. His tastes were eclectic because he was exposed to music somewhat at random. He saw albums at a second-hand store and bought them many times because he liked the cover, or they were cheap. Consequently, Kurt had no idea that the Knack were considered uncool by most punk rockers. In that innocence, he absorbed their pop sound. He invited a friend over that year, sat him down saying he had a great album to play, and put on *Get the Knack*. The friend thought Kurt was joking. Would that pop influence have soaked in if Kurt read Pitchfork.com and realized how unhip his then-favorite band was? Would Kurt have even written "Smells Like Teen Spirit" if he'd searched the name on Google and realized he was writing an anthem to a teenage girl's deodorant? Would early negative online reviews have scuttled the career of someone with an ego as tremendously fragile as his? And, the biggest question of all, could a band like Nirvana ever exist again, starting as a slow build, a secret discovery, touring in a van as unknowns, writing great songs because there was no money to be made from the Seattle club scene, writing lyrics and journal entries on paper for hours and hours, jumping from college radio to the mainstream and, eventually, long after they'd logged in their ten thousand hours of live performance, four years after they began, *finally* break through and dominate every single radio format? Or would today's Kurt Cobain see a negative review on Facebook and hang it all up after he earned only ten likes?

Kurt had no idea music and culture would change so much, but he knew that to make a lasting impact he had to create a singular vision. He said as much in his journals: "So after figuring out songs like the Troggs' 'Wild Thing,' and the Cars' 'My Best Friend's Girl,' I decided that in order to become a big, famous rock star I would need to write my very own songs instead of wasting my time learning other people's, because if you study other people's music too much, it may act as an obstruction on developing your own personal style . . .

"I guess what I'm trying to say is: Theory is a waste of time. Too much practice is like too much sugar."

★ ★ ★

Kurt's influence went beyond just fans or music critics or best-of-list makers; he inspired musicians, writers, and artists. Some were novelists, some were painters, but most were musicians. You could craft a book just out of comments other rock stars have made about Kurt.

Noel Gallagher, to *Guitar World*: "The only person I have any respect for as a songwriter over the last ten years is Kurt Cobain. He was the perfect cross between Lennon and McCartney."

PJ Harvey, to Barney Hoskyns: "As a writer, I had enormous respect for him. He was an incredible writer and an incredible singer . . . He was one of those special people. There was a light inside him that you could see. He had a charisma that went beyond his physical presence."

Patti Smith, to me: "I loved Nirvana and Kurt. I really could relate to his lyrics; I could feel them. He put every bit of himself into those songs, and that's always the challenge of any artist."

Pete Townshend, in *The Observer*: "Nirvana's second album, *Nevermind,* was a breath of 'punk' fresh air in the musically stale early nineties."

Neil Young, to *Mojo*: "He really, really inspired me. He was so great. Wonderful. One of the best, but more than that. Kurt was one of the absolute best all time for me."

David Bowie, to *Spin*: "I was simply blown away when

I found out that Kurt Cobain liked my work, and I always wanted to talk to him about his reasons for covering 'The Man Who Sold the World.' It was a good straightforward rendition and sounded somehow very honest. It would have been nice to have worked with him, but just talking would have been real cool."

Vernon Reid, of Living Color, in *Rolling Stone*: "Cobain changed the course of where the music went. There are certain people where you can see the axis of musical history twisting on them: Hendrix was pivotal, Prince was pivotal, Cobain was pivotal."

Bruce Springsteen, to *Guitar World*: "[Nirvana] changed everything. They opened a vein of freedom that didn't exist previously. Kurt Cobain did something very similar to what Dylan did in the sixties, which was to sound different and get on the radio. He proved that a guitarist could sound different and still be heard. So Cobain reset a lot of very fundamental rules, and that type of artist is very few and far between."

Bono, to *Newsweek*: "I remember watching Kurt come through and thinking, 'God, this music is nuclear.' This is really splitting the atom. They raised the temperature for everybody. Manufactured pop never looked so cold as when that heat was around."

Bob Dylan, on the radio: "That kid has heart."

Michael Stipe, to *Newsweek*: "I know what the next Nirvana recording was going to sound like. It was going to be very quiet and acoustic, with lots of stringed instruments. It was going to be an amazing fucking record, and I'm a little bit angry at him for killing himself. He and I were going to record a trial run of the album, a demo tape. It was all set up. He had a plane ticket. He had a car picking him up. And at the last minute he called, and said, 'I can't come.'"

Dave Grohl, to *NME*: "I still dream about Kurt. Every time I see him in a dream, I'll be amazed and I get this feeling that everyone else thinks he's dead. It always feels totally real, probably because I'm a very vivid dreamer. But, in my dreams, Kurt's usually been hiding—we'll get together and I'll end up asking him, 'God, where have you been?'"

Krist Novoselic, to me: "[Music] is the most important thing about Kurt; not his death. The details of his death are just lurid . . . Kurt was expressive. His heart was his receiver and his transmitter . . . He expressed himself in a highly creative and compelling way, and it's affected so many people."

Courtney Love, to me in 1999: "My favorite thing of Kurt's was a sheet he had where he'd written out his top bands, his top fifty. One of the things I liked about him was that he was a collector, but he didn't collect the things I did at all. He had no Bunnymen, no Hüsker Dü. There's no Replacements, no Big Star. It's just Saints, Sabbath. It's Big Black and Black Flag. It's Saccharine Trust and Celtic Frost. It's 'man music.' His favorite R.E.M. record was *Green*. No way does he go back [into R.E.M.'s catalog] for 'Perfect Circle,' or 'Catapult.' There were a couple of things he learned from people in Olympia about 'cutie music.' That's on there too: [like] Jad Fair.

"He couldn't fucking tell you who Julian Cope was. Once we were driving around Los Angeles listening to KROQ, and 'Killing Moon' came on, and I love that song. And he said, 'You just like that romantic music.' And I said, 'Yeah, and you like Saccharine Trust, punker-boy.'"

Courtney Love, to me in 2000: "I think *Nevermind* made older people feel young. It put them in touch with their sixties and seventies sense of rebellion."

Me: "My argument has always been that *Nevermind* was a success because the emotion of the songs was so apparent, even without the lyrics."

Courtney Love: "Exactly. But a lot of things happened subsequent to that album coming out—all the other signings of bands, the stampede, the [Grunge] phenomenon—and people forgot that it really was the songs. And the magic. You connect with an audience when you have magic, when your voice connects with a listener. And Kurt had that magic."

Courtney Love, to me in 2002, about Kurt's legacy: "In our society, art and celebrity has everything to do with being untapped. Do you think Nirvana would still be vital today? I say abso-fucking-lutely. Janis Joplin was done. Jim Morrison was done. Jimi Hendrix was done. But Kurt, he wasn't done. You are talking about somebody, at twenty-seven, who had barely scratched the surface."

Courtney Love, to me, 2003, on Frances Bean Cobain: "She's got great karma. And she's just such a great human. And it's really important that she came here [and was born]. And it's really important that she not get the load dumped on her that Sean [Lennon] did. You never know if you are going to like your kids, but I'm honored she's my daughter, our daughter."

No analysis of Kurt Cobain could ever be complete enough to encompass every aspect of his legacy. The question of any performer's impact is ultimately a personal one. If you were touched or moved in any way by Kurt Cobain, whatever drew you in is the key to what that legacy means to you now. There are as many answers to Larry King's query—"Why did Kurt Cobain matter?"—as there are Nirvana fans.

There is, however, one physical embodiment of Kurt's legacy beyond just his albums, and that, of course, is Frances Bean Cobain. She is a twenty-one-year-old as I write this book. She now controls aspects of Kurt's estate and will have a say in the future how his tangible assets are marketed. She has Kurt's striking blue eyes, and she's gorgeous, a mix of the best features of her two parents. She's lived with a troubled family history and has had to deal with remarkable intrusions to her privacy as well. I've heard a few stories over the years of disrespectful strangers who have literally grabbed Frances and announced they wanted to "touch" Kurt. The first time this ever happened, Courtney told me, was backstage at *Saturday Night Live*, and the person grabbing then–baby Frances was a B-list movie star who you would have thought would have known better. But it has happened in all sorts of places, including once at the ballet when Frances was seven and an elderly, matronly woman grabbed Frances away from Courtney and said, "I want to look into the eyes of Kurt Cobain." In a *People* magazine piece, Frances called these encounters "creepy" and said she is quick to note to anyone, "I'm not my parents." She does, however, have a sense of humor and understands irony and serendipity, two of the main ingredients to her father's success.

Last year, Frances was walking through a large comic-book convention wearing a cardigan sweater. A stranger approached her. This happens all the time to beautiful and famous young women, but in this instance the man who approached her clearly had no idea who he was talking to. He probably was trying to hit on her. He looked at her outfit and remarked, "Pretty good Kurt Cobain imitation."

I didn't see this incident firsthand, so I can only imagine the expression on Frances's face, how her eyes would have skirted around as she tried to comprehend exactly what was being said, whether the guy was a stalker, another creep, or just a random dude trying to get her number. Somehow in my mind I imagine Frances's look at the moment the rich irony of this came to her, and I imagine it would have looked remarkably similar to what I saw on her father's face back in September 1991, pre-fame, pre-Frances, when he and the other members of Nirvana were getting kicked out of their own Seattle record-release party for *Nevermind* for starting a food fight.

★ ★ ★

This book touches on only a handful of the ways Kurt affected music and culture—the ways I saw as most significant or easiest to track. Kurt appealed to people for many reasons, and continues to do so, and most parts of that are not as quantifiable as Nirvana's album sales, the amount of radio airplay he earned, or the number of sneakers that have his name on them. To most people his impact is personal, and it will be different for everyone.

Over the years many fans, seeking more information on ways they felt they intersected with Kurt, have contacted me. Those have included some who wanted to know more about his left-handedness, and how that variance affected his creativity, but many seem to share some kind of medical issue with Kurt. Often they ask if I know if he was ever diagnosed with some kind of malady they have, for example manic depression (he was never officially diagnosed, as far I know). Sometimes they share one of the issues he most certainly had: scoliosis, irritable bowel syndrome, ADHD, drug addiction. Kurt had so many health problems that his story connects with a panoply of people with similar ailments.

I can't help these people in their quest for further information because Kurt's myriad medical issues were never well documented. I examined some of his medical records that still exist and spoke with a few of his physicians, but given the chaos of his life, it wasn't exactly like he was carting around a file folder of his patient records. Still, I found it fascinating when I discovered that Kurt's stomach problems were so unique, and so pathological, that his case is still discussed in medical schools—minus his name on the records, of course. If Kurt were alive, this fact might give him more satisfaction than his ranking on any rock critic's best-of list: that medical students at this very moment might be pouring over X-rays of his stomach and trying to figure out his ailments. Kurt wrote in his journal once that he wanted his own disease named after him. In a way, that's come true.

But sometimes even thinking about Kurt's medical problems makes me feel melancholy, simply because there's a sadness in armchair quarterbacking a life that has already been lost. I'm nearly certain that if Kurt had been treated with a medical "whole body" approach—with all his issues tackled by a talented team—his drug addiction may have been easier to beat once his other problems were in check. Kurt's lifelong stomach ailments caused him the greatest physical pain in his life, and when he discovered that opiates helped block that hurt, his addiction never receded for long. There are so many what-ifs in the story of a man who dies young and tragically.

There are no answers, no matter how many hours you spend pondering, no matter how long you dream. Events of history don't change just because you wonder about them, or Larry King asks a thousand what-ifs.

When you wake up from your dream, that haunting red Line One button is still flashing, still waiting for you.

And he's still gone.

ACKNOWLEDGMENTS

Special thanks go to Carrie Thornton (who like me has Bunnymen albums next to punk-rock ones), and Sarah Lazin (pretty fine classic-album collection as well) for the steerage on this project. Other support came from Cal Morgan, Brittany Hamblin, Doug Manelski, Manuela Jessel, Heidi Metcalfe Lewis, Lorie Pagnozzi, and the rest of the staff at It Books and HarperCollins. For help with research or interviews within the world of Nirvana—on this project and past ones—I'd like to acknowledge the assistance of Ryan Aigner, Cortney Alexander, Mark Arm, Joris Baas, Skip Berger, Jim Berkenstadt, Lauren Brown, Aaron Burckhard, Jeff Burlingame, David Byrnes, Nicole Jon Carroll, Chad Channing, Marco Collins, Stephanie Coontz, Kurt Danielson, Marie Walsh Dixon, Mike Doughty, Mari Earl, Jasen Emmons, Jack Endino, Steve Fisk, Gillian Gaar, Cam Garret, Dave Grohl, Rasmus Holmen, Mitch Holmquist, John Hughes, Robert Hunter, David Jobes, Chaz Kangas, Stephanie Kuehnert, Erica Krusen, Andrea Linett, Courtney Love, Tracy

Marander, Jacob McMurray, Michael Meisel, Krist Novoselic, Harold Owens, Bruce Pavitt, Jonathan Poneman, Charles Peterson, Hilary Richrod, Pepper Schwartz, Ava Stander, Susie Tennant, Kim Thayil, Vicki Wagner, Alice Wheeler, and Mike Ziegler.

I'd also like to thank my family, including Ashland Cross, Bettie Cross, Catherine Cross, Herb Cross, Joe Guppy, John Keister, Brenda Lane, Geoff MacPherson, Carl Miller, Matt Smith, and Sarah Westbook. Thanks also go to Ken Anderson, Will Balla, Erik Bell, Julie Cascioppo, Peter Callaghan, Amber Caska, Aaron Coberly, Caspian Coberly, Mary Crandall, Paul DeBarros, Don Desantis, Melissa Duane, David Dubois, Sue Ennis, Cathy Erickson, Erik Flannigan, Wayne Foster, David French, Ray Rae Goldman, Nancy Guppy, Robert Hilburn, Josh Jacobson, Larry Jacobson, Dwight Jacobson, Eric Johnson, Bill King, Mary Kohl, John Kohl, Chris Kornelis, Gretchen Lauber, Joe Lee, Arthur Levin, Ben London, Cindy May, Summer Mayne, Norman McGlashan, Lance Mercer, Curtis Minato, Barbara Mitchell, Marshall Nelson, Mark Nuckols, Michael O'Mahony, Harley O'Neil Jr., Don O'Neill, Shannon Payne, Peter Philbin, Chris Phillips, Ed Pierson, Rebecca Polinsky, Jonathan Pont, the staff of *The Rocket* (1979–2000, R.I.P.), Bob Rivers, Craig Rosenberg, Mary Schuh (R.I.P.), Shinkle Family, Megan Snyder-Camp, Denise Sullivan, Sam Sutherland, Charley Sweet,

Brad Tolinski, Mary Truscott, Ron Upshaw, Mary Anne Vance, Michael Wansley, Cynthia West, Ann Wilson, Nancy Wilson, Amely Wurmbrand, and, of course, Larry King, without whom this book wouldn't have had a beginning.

This book addressed the impact of the life and work of someone who died way too young, because of many complications. If you or someone you know needs assistance with mental health or addiction issues, there are resources are available. There are free addiction and recovery support groups in virtually every city in the United States, and the only requirement for attendance is a desire to break the habit. The MusiCares MAP Fund is one group that provides specific assistance for musicians or those in the music industry in need of addiction-recovery services (Musicares.org, 1-800-687-4227). In the field of suicide prevention, there are many resources available, and the Centers for Disease Control and Prevention lists many on their website (cdc.gov/violence prevention/suicide/). The American Foundation for Suicide Prevention (AFSP) maintains a twenty-four-hour hotline (1-800-273-TALK). Every year the AFSP holds walkathons in hundreds of cities around the United States to raise funds and increase awareness about this national health crisis. There is help.

APRIL 13 · APRIL 27, 1994   *Free and Available Every Other Wednesday*